MURDER IN WASHINGTON
Notorious Washington Murder Sites

marques vickers

MURDER IN WASHINGTON
Notorious Washington Murder Sites

By Marques Vickers

**MARQUIS PUBLISHING
HERRON ISLAND, WASHINGTON**

@2016-2021 Marques Vickers

All rights reserved. Copyright under Berne Copyright Convention, Universal Copyright Convention, and Pan-American Copyright Convention. No part of this book may be reproduced, stored in a retrieval system, or transmitted in any form, or by any means, electronic, mechanical, photocopying, recording, or otherwise, without prior permission of the author or publisher.

Version 1.3

Published by Marquis Publishing
Herron Island, Washington

Vickers, Marques, 1957

Dedicated to my daughters Charline and Caroline

SOURCES AND ARCHIVES SOURCED

The Spokesman-Review, The Seattle Times, The Renton Reporter, The News Tribune, The Daily Chronicle of Centralia, The Daily World, Daily Record News, Seattle Post-Intelligencer, Peninsula Daily News, The Herald, The Daily News, The Olympian, Kitsap Sun, Aberdeen Herald, Spokane Daily Chronicle, The Stranger, The Columbian, , Murderpedia.org, Wikipedia.org, FindACase.com, Doc.Wa.gov/offenderinfo, StalkingSeattle.Blogspot.com, HistoryLink.org, CharleyProject.org, Daily Kos, New York Times, Willamette Week, Coeur d'Alene Press, Los Angeles Times, The Atlantic Magazine, New Yorker Magazine, Sequim Gazette, South China Morning Post, Wikiwand.com, University of Washington Library, TacomaPublicLibrary.org, Forejustice.org, WashingtonHistoryOnline.org, Everett Public Library, Yakima Valley Museum, Gorgenewscenter.com, Newstalkit.com, TheNorthwest.com, NWSource.com, NWGangs.proboard, SpokaneValleyOnline.com, CrimeWiseUSA.com, TheEscapist.com, OregonLive.com, Highbeam.com, BlinkOnCrime.com, Sandpoint.com, Vietnamwar.OurWarHeroes.org, FBI.gov, MyNorthwest.com, SeattleMet.com, FreeRepublic.com, CapitolHill.com, HeraldNet.com, KPLU.org, TheInvisibleJuror.com, Highbeam.com, StalkingVictims.com, LivingSnoqualmic.com, SeattlePoliceGuild.org, Heavy.com, Modernnotion.com, SeattleMet.com, Topix.com, StarvationHeights.com, CrimeWiseUSA.com, TheTruckersReport.com, CrimeMuseum.org, Facebook, PureIntimacy.com Bellinghamherald.com and Kitsapsun.com.

Photography shot between 2019-2021. Some of the locations may have altered with time and ownership changes. Many of the locations are still privately inhabited. Please don't disturb the residents.

Table of Contents:

Assassinations

Doug Carlile: The Unrealized Oil Field Killing For Hire
Edwin Pratt: A Civil Rights Assassination or Political Rival Killing?
Laura Law: The Bludgeoning A Child of an Ethnic Labor Movement
Tom Wales: The Perfect Assassination?
A Manipulated Killing By A Simpleton

Historical Legacies

Ann Marie Burr: A Mother's Torment of Never Knowing Her Daughter's Fate
The Floating Fleet of Billy Ghol
The Centralia Parade March and Massacre
The Unsolved Kidnapping of Young Charles F. Mattson
Chief Leschi's Execution: A Legacy of Shame
Fred Ross Ring Death: The Inherent Dangers of Exhibition Fighting
Everett Dockside Massacre: Sunday Bloody Sunday
Sylvia Gaines: The Final Vestiges of Scandal Has Been Removed
West Seattle Bridge: A Collision With An Unanticipated Destiny
Murderous Revenge Spawned By The *Brides of Christ* Cult
People's Theatre: The Legacy of Seattle's Private Female Performers and Police Chief Killer

Chance Encounters and Impulse Killings

David Lee Childs: An Aesthetic Violated By Vulgarity
Delbert Belton: The Savage Beating of an Elderly World War II Veteran

John Anthony Castro: A Careless and Violent Lifestyle with Predictable Consequences
The Brief Extinguished Flame of Recording Artist Little Willie John
Mia Zapata and the Randomly Silenced Voice of the Street
The Abruptly Silenced Voice of Radio Activist Mike Webb
The Weighty Complexity In Executing Killer Mitchell Rupe
Nathan Trigger Gilstrap: The Gangland Intrusion Into Our Neighborhood Fortresses
Patrick Gibson: A Tainted Hat Nearly Undermines A Cold Case Conviction
Two Child Killers Separated By City Blocks and DNA Profiles
Edward Scott McMichael: The Silencing of A Whimsical Tune
William Batten: A Lifetime of Sexual Abuse Provoked Incarceration
Alex Baranyi and David Anderson: The Thrill of the Kill
A Fatal Stabbing Of One of Society's Forgotten
Maternal Homicide Based on a One-Sided Werewolf Attack

Unsolved Murders

Marsha Weatter and Katherine Allen: Mount St. Helens Ash Buries Two Hitchhiking Shooting Victims
The Forgotten Unsolved Killing of Louis Bellessa
The Invisible Streetwalkers Along Tacoma's Puyallup Avenue
Oleg Babichenko: An Explosion Prompting A Response of Silence
Roseanne Pleasant and Valiree Jackson: The Dual Generation Probable Killing of A Mother and Daughter
Susette Werner's Unimaginable Early Morning Dragging Death

Timothy Alioth and Donna Plew: A Double Homicide Mystery Within A Residential Oasis
Chalisa Lewis: The Vanishing of a Young Poetic Soul
Fred Cohen: The Perfectly Executed Murder of A Preeminent Local Attorney
A Surprising Suspect Emerges Amidst the Embers of A Cold Case Murder

Rampage Murders

A Very Public Suicide on the Notorious Aurora Bridge
Collective Grieving, Renewal and Hope Following An Unexplainable Rampage at the Café Racer
No One is Welcome in This Jungle
Michael Feeney: His Fateful and Tragic Obsession
Ali Muhammad Brown: Using Religious Fanaticism As A Pretext For Unspeakable Acts
James William Cushing: The Vulnerability of a Fractured Mind
John Alkins: Crossing Professional Boundaries Into Extremities
John Fiori: The Eruption and Rage of an Invisible Individual
Kyle Huff: The Capital Hill Massacre
The Marysville-Pilchuck High School Shooting: A Familiar Scenario Targeted Towards Atypical Victims
Michael Harmon: A Contender In The Dumbest Homicide Possible Competition
A Street Culture Slaying Resembling A Traditional Murder
The Red Barn Door Tavern Massacre: The Reformation of A Vicious Mass Killer?
Aaron Ybarra: A School Shooting Prefaced By A Living Hell
The Man of A Thousand Identities
Jennifer Hopper: Devine Forgiveness for an Unpardonable Act

Zachary Craven: The Devalued Exchange of Human Life
Premeditated Murders

The Anderson Family Killings: Three Generations Lost on Christmas Eve
The Charles Goldmark Family Murder: Erroneous Presumptions
Barrett Bailey: Vanished and Renamed But Never Too Far Removed From Suspicion
The Murder Experiment that Concluded Dreadfully Wrong
James Elledge: A Rare Example of Legitimate Remorse?
Jed Waits: Destroying the Infatuation He Could Not Possess
Jeremy McLean: The Revenge Killing of A Drug Informant
Naveed Afzal Haq's Lone Rampage Against American Foreign Policy
The Dredged Trunk Recovery: Seattle's Mahoney Disappearance Scandal
Pang Frozen Food Fire: An Empire of Achievement Devoured In An Evening's Flames
Patrick Drum: A Self-Appointed One Man Hit Squad Against Sexual Predators
Peter Keller: The Survivalist Killer Who Ultimately Couldn't Hide
Rafay Family Murders: The Damning Conversations That Sabotaged A Perfect Alibi
The Detonation of Samuel Lau's Demons
An Asian Gangland Slaying During A Turbulent Tacoma Era
Wah Mee Gambling Club: A Massacre That Shook The Foundations of An Illegal Seattle Tradition
A Murder-Suicide Leaving A Perpetrator in Purgatory
Sex Offender Slaying Defines A Lone Vigilante Crusade

Law Enforcement Related Fatalities

Maurice Clemmons: A Lifetime of Debauchery Ends in Unnecessary Sacrifice For Four Policemen
Niles Meservey Death: A Homicidal Impatience By One of the Good Guys
Timothy Brenton: A Police Officer Ambush Motivated By Extreme Hatred
Officer Volney Stevens: An Open Season On Shooting Seattle Policemen
Otto Zehm: An Overzealous Killing of A Simple Man

Serial Killings and Killers

Donna Perry: Assigning Gender Accountability For Past Actions
George Russell, Jr.: Outsider and Sadistic Serial Killing
Gary Ridgway: The Green River Executioner Appearing As Evil Incarnate
The Fatal Curse of Jake Bird
The Vile Pride of Child Killer Joe Kondro
Lee Malvo: An Assassination Dictated By Subservience
Morris Frampton: The Beast and the Banality of Darkness
Robert Lee Yates: Washington's Dead Man Walking Pleads for Another Unmerited Extension of Life
Rodney Alcala: A Beastly Killing Machine Slaying Beauty
Linda Burfield Hazzard: A Barbaric Medical Practitioner Dispensing Lethal Salt and Water
Warren Forest: A Heart of Darkness Permanently Confined From Society
Ted Bundy: The Man Who Lived To Kill Women
Kenneth Bianchi: Over Forty Years of Time Remaining Stationary For An Unrepentant Killer

About The Author

Preface: Murder in the Evergreen State of Washington

Murder is often a tragically intended attempt to separate the living into darkness by violent means. This pitch-blackness may be the sole existence and misery a perpetrator has known their entire lives.

Some killings defy explanation and understanding. Some may not properly be defined as evil. For the innocent victims of homicides, their stilled voices are silenced, but their identities and stories should never be forgotten. Not all of the victims profiled in this edition were innocent.

Whatever the orientation of the culprit, victim or circumstances, trauma accompanies each loss. The taint behind a killing remains fresh to the immediate victim's families, friends and diverse relationships. The ghosts of recollection are prevalent, searing and painful. They never entirely recede within a lifetime.

My introduction to the consequences of murder began with the December 20, 1968 killings of David Faraday and Betty Lou Jensen by the Zodiac killer. The shocking executions were committed on an isolated stretch of Lake Herman Road near the city limits of my hometown, Vallejo, California. I was acquainted with Faraday through my involvement with Boy Scouts. My older sister knew both of the victims.

One cannot forget the trauma a random double homicide inflicts upon an intimate suburban community. Seven months later, the same killer attacked a couple in the parking lot of a local park all of us had frequented since childhood. One victim survived but the Zodiac's death toll was mounting. He would be responsible for at least two additional deaths and another surviving victim. His evil became personal.

The cowardly murderer publicly taunted law enforcement authorities and the citizenry via the news media. He was never apprehended. Abruptly we realized that Vallejo had changed. Our illusions of invulnerability were permanently destroyed. The reputation of the city of Vallejo would continue its decline over time and acts of senseless violence would become more commonplace.

It is often difficult to feel empathy for perpetrators. Detachment remains difficult when so many have suffered. They are responsible for substantial loss and yet many offer no remorse. The acknowledgement of the victims often pales in comparison with the exposure of the murderers. The Washington State justice system rarely judges the guilty expediently. The death penalty is scarcely employed, mocking its role as a deterrent.

Within the context of examining each profile, many important issues are raised for discussion without necessarily culminating in resolution. These subjects include capital punishment, American racial perceptions, parental influences, child rearing, media reporting, public bias, juvenile sentencing, self-incrimination protections and the impartiality of our judicial system. Controversial options such as voluntary euthanasia for the condemned are suggested when examining the hopeless backlog of death row and life-term convicts.

Capturing snapshots of fatality locations is never precise. There are news accounts, historical images, but much of the precise identification is speculative. Visual location often adds perspective to a profile narrative.

Crime scenes typically revert back into unremarkable landscape or unassuming buildings over the ensuing years and decades. Several have altered little since their moment of infamy. Many are passed daily by pedestrian and vehicular traffic unaware of a location's unique significance.

Makeshift on-site memorials often temporarily acknowledge the stain and the loss. Few remain permanently. Instead, layers of paint, building facade modifications and even address changes attempt to camouflage many crime scenes. The disguises are understandable. Those condemned to live amongst the lingering shadows of a tragedy sometimes become victims themselves in a sense. Society wishes to forget and move on. Murder is never tidy. Remembrance is inconvenient and uncomfortable for the living.

My hope is that these profiles and images will honor the innocent who are no longer amongst us.

Doug Carlile: The Unrealized Oil Field Killing For Hire

On the evening of December 15, 2013, Doug and Elberta Carlile returned to their upscale Spokane South Hill neighborhood home. Elberta mounted the staircase to their bedroom. An armed man clad in black and wearing gloves confronted Doug in the kitchen.

Carlile, 63, was likely certain he was to be killed although he was unfamiliar with his assailant. As his wife began descending the staircase, he repeatedly addressed the gunman with the words *Don't do anything*. He knew his request was pointless but hoped the elevated tone of his voice would serve as a warning to his wife to remain upstairs. His intent succeeded. Elberta hid in her bedroom closet fearing the worst.

Carlile's request was followed by seven shots. The echos resounded throughout the house. Afterwards, Doug Carlile lay dead on the kitchen floor. Investigators recovered multiple casing from the scene and several stray bullets. One was lodged in a kitchen wall and another inside a popcorn popper. Two handguns were also discovered. His killer opted to flee rather than scour the house for witnesses. He left fresh footprints from the Carlile's backyard mud directed towards a nearby elementary school.

Once the house fell silent, Elberta telephoned police. A sighting of a suspicious white van was registered on a surveillance camera at the nearby school.

One month later, police arrested Timothy Suckow on suspicion of murder. Suckow's apprehension was prompted by the police discovery of his van apparently parked in plain view outside of his Spokane Valley home. Despite a citywide description of the vehicle, he had never bothered to dispose of it.

Investigators discovered an even more incredulous finding. Inside his personal pick-up truck was a murder checklist itemizing numerous items and actions required for the killing. DNA evidence from a leather glove left in the backyard of the crime scene matched Suckow's. His sloppiness as an assassin would have shamed the profession.

His personal background proved disturbing. He had previously been incarcerated in jails and mental health institutions in Minnesota, California and New Mexico. He had been diagnosed with a range of mental issues including bipolar disorder, depression and substance abuse. He was recorded to have complained about demonic possession and attempted suicide on multiple occasions.

Tracing such a dubious choice of professional to its source proved elemental. Why was such an unreliable individual hired?

The background behind the killing proved murkier than the black crude prospecting that prompted it. Doug Carlile's complex business dealings in North Dakota reservation based oil wells was both confusing and his undoing.

Prior to his death, Carlile had solicited hundred of thousands of dollars from several investors to purchase Indian reservation land with the potential to produce billions of dollars worth of crude. The prospects never matched the proceeds. One of his early investors James Henrikson was enraged by his absence of a financial return.

Carlile owned 51% of a company called Kingdom

Dynamics that held mineral rights to 640 acres on the Mandan Hidatsa and Arikara Nation Reservation. His operations also included construction equipment hauling.

How legitimate was his operation and investment prospective?

Henrikson claimed that Carlile owed him $1.88 million. Other sources indicated that the project had gone nowhere as Carlile was having difficulty getting his overall financing in order. Was this merely a temporary delay or a planned strategy?

Hendrickson was anxious about his investment. Sources indicated he was demanding nearly a half-million dollars from Carlile, payable immediately. Another account by the district attorney prosecuting the case indicated that Carlile would not give up his shares in an oil lease to Hendrickson on the Fort Berthold Indian Reservation. Whether Carlile actually owed him nearly $2 million was never clearly determined.

Hendrickson had made threats against Carlile's family. Doug Carlile had a premonition about his own fate. He advised one son that should he be killed one day, Henrikson would be the responsible party. As the intensity of threats escalated and business relations deteriorated, another of Carlile's son loaned a gun to him for protection. He was unarmed when he was killed.

Hendrickson was the prime suspect for ordering the killing from the beginning. Police telephoned him two hours after the shooting. He vehemently denied involvement. When Suckow the assassin, was arrested, his cell phone included Hendrickson's direct number.

Around the time of Suckow's detainment, Henrikson was arrested in Watford City, North Dakota on weapons charges. Only 36, his personal background was dark and unsavory. He had multiple felony convictions in Oregon and was connected to numerous scams and unscrupulous business dealings. Everyone and everything connected to him reeked of suspicion. His web of intrigue included the February 2012 disappearance of an employee, Kristopher Clarke. A body was never recovered, but Suckow was ultimately linked to the disappearance and killing.

The case took a weirder turn when in April 2014, Robby Wahrer, 33, was arrested for having driven the getaway van on the evening of Carlile's killing. His name was also included on Suckow's cell phone directory. He had been convicted of eight prior felonies and most recently arrested for selling methamphetamines. A warrant had been issued for his arrest four days before the shooting for missing a court appearance.

Wahrer provided unintentional comic relief to a sobering tale when he indicated that the victim was only supposed to have his legs or kneecaps broken. His delusion of *Mafioso* tactics proved as farcical as an event on August 2015, while Henrikson was awaiting trial at the Spokane County jail.

Scriptwriters could not image a more hackneyed plot when the imprisoned Henrikson and his cellmate attempted to escape the jail by dangling a rope composed of tied bedsheets to a dumpster on the ground level. The line was easily detected. Worse, the spacing gap between bars on the windows was no wider than a cellular phone.

Henrikson was transferred to the Yakima County jail two weeks later.

The sordid trial proved less entertaining. All of the directly involved and three periphery parties pleaded guilty to their respective roles. James Henrikson was sentenced to forty years for ordering the killings of Carlile and Clarke and is currently incarcerated at the USP Penitentiary in Pollock, Louisiana. Timothy Suckow was sentenced to thirty years for performing both killings and remains at FCI Fairton Federal Penitentiary in Fairton, New Jersey. Robby Wahrer, the getaway driver, was sentenced to ten years and is currently serving his sentence at the USP Atwater, California. Lazaro Pesina, who was prepared to break in to the Carlile's home with Suckow was sentenced to twelve years and is interned at FCI Safford in Safford, Arizona. Robert Delao, who was a key witness against Hendrickson in Carliles's death as well as the disappearance of Clarke received a thirty year sentence in spite of his critical testimony.. The judge factored in Delao's lengthy criminal history, which also included another murder. He is presently imprisoned at FCI Otisville in Otisville, New York.

Amidst the maze of conflicting stories tied to the case, Doug Carlile's ethical reputation was repeatedly questioned. He is in no position to defend his integrity. His family has maintained his innocence and honor throughout.

But the obvious question remains. What happened to the investor's monies? The question has never been satisfactorily resolved.

In November 2018, a Watford City, North Dakota accountant Rene L. Johnson was convicted of wire fraud for a 2013 high-risk loan of $400,000 she had provided to Kingdom Dyamics before Carlile's death without informing her clients. The jury found her *not guilty* of three additional charges. The loan was based on a guarantee of doubling her money in 90 days. The return never materialized but Johnson was later reimbursed with interest after she had threatened Carlile and Hendrickson with a lawsuit. Johnson was sentenced to 100 hours of community service, but no prison time in March 2019.

The business falling out between Henrikson's investment and Carlile's purported promises disintegrated into a matter of unrealized financial expectations. What ultimately transpired between them and if Carlile was partially to blame will probably never adequately be sorted out.

The allure of untapped oil resources has remained an elusive investment for speculators for decades. The past decades discovery of resources on previous virgin territory has created a boom environment on previously impoverished land. Wealth, greed and inflated hopes have accompanied the promise. Doug Carlile paid a fateful price when he was unable to deliver to one exasperated investor.

**Doug Carlile's Murder Site:
2505 South Garfield Road, Spokane**

A Civil Rights Assassination or Political Rival Killing?

The roots of the American Civil Rights movement have been principally credited to the southern American states. The battles for racial equality, however were fought nationally and often under the radar of media exposure.

Edwin Pratt was considered one of Seattle's most prominent African-American spokespersons during the 1960s. He had risen through the organizational ranks to become the director of the Urban League of Metropolitan Seattle.

By 1969, a year following the assassination of Martin Luther King Jr., his idealism had become pragmatic. The organization's emphasis was oriented towards school and workplace desegregation, upgrading racially concentrated neighborhoods and ending police harassment. He was considered a moderate, admired for his sense of humor and ability to negotiate fairly with divergent viewpoints.

His conciliatory approach made him popular within leadership circles, but alienated him from more extreme racially biased perspectives and individuals. He received angry letters, intimidating messages and periodic threats on his life, even at public meetings.

His legacy remains the dichotomy of a turbulent era in American racial relations. There was marginal ground for a middle stance as sides polarized the issues. The contradiction remains today with high-profile racial representatives and activists. To sustain support, they must often remain ideologically dogmatic, despite the fact that society has changed significantly. The landscape and evolution continues and remains far from simplistic.

Edwin Pratt was not a simple personality. His world demanded balancing professional and personal conflict on a teetering equilibrium.

He was married for 13 years to his wife Bettye and had a 5-year old daughter. Rumors persisted that the marriage was unstable and that he was having an affair with his secretary, who was Caucasian. Further speculation indicated he was looking to make a professional change and possibly enter the ranks of private enterprise.

On the evening of January 26, 1969, Seattle suffered a freak snowstorm disabling roadways and keeping many residents housebound. Pratt had settled in for the evening with his family. He heard sounds resembling snowballs hitting his Rambler parked outside. Bettye was tucking their daughter into bed. Pratt, wearing slippers, stuck his head out of the front door upon viewing figures in his driveway carport.

His enquiry of *Who's there?* elicited a shotgun blast that ripped him apart. The slug tore through his mouth and lodged in his neck after glancing off bone, severing his spine. He died instantly. Two figures disappeared into the frigid night in a waiting car. Neighbors who did view the suspects were unclear as to their age or even race.

The killing initially prompted national attention and substantial investigation both locally and by the FBI. The investigation finally evaporated despite a substantial reward. Over the years, the cold case was resuscitated and fresh suspects emerged. No one was ever charged with his death. None of the prominent suspects remain alive.

Among the two most credible theories was 1) a killing for hire arranged by an African American contractor resentful of Pratt's politics and 2) three low-level racists thugs targeting a prominent African-American figure. One Seattle newspaper connected the two divergent parties together based on the killing-for-hire scenario.

Dead men can no longer be punished for their transgressions anymore than truth is revealed through sealed mouths. Speculation and rumor become the bitter consolation for a grieving widow and daughter.

Many who neither sought the recognition nor consequences with their demise became the front line soldiers and icons in the struggle for racial equality. Pratt's legacy is scarcely mentioned in the national historical dialogue. His role however, remains important since the higher middle ground changes he sought are necessary for a balanced society. It is idealistic to assume that evolutions in racial, gender and sexual preferences can be universally realized in a single generation.

Individuals such as Edwin Pratt realized that forward progress is earned by small victories. His vision, patience and foresight sadly was misunderstood by extremists and their tunneled vision perspectives affecting a society composed of many races. In 1976, Edwin T. Pratt Park was named in his honor. The park is bounded by 20th Avenue S, Yesler Way and 18th Avenue S in Seattle.

**Edwin Pratt's Murder Site:
17916 1st Avenue NE, Seattle**

Laura Law: The Bludgeoning A Child of an Ethnic Labor Movement

Nearly three years before the Pearl Harbor bombing incited America's entry in World War II, the global conflict prompted numerous domestic skirmishes.

On the evening of January 5, 1940, someone entered the Aberdeen home of Dick and Laura Law and bludgeoned Laura to death with an ice pick in their living room. Domestic violence is typically suspected when a young mother is murdered in her own residence. Indeed, Dick Law was immediately considered the prime suspect.

The Laws however were not your typical small town married couple of the era. Laura Law was not a prototype housewife.

In 1935, Laura married Dick Law, an International Woodworkers of America union executive board member. Lumber was the commercial artery of Aberdeen. Relations between the unions and lumber companies were extremely contentious. The Laws were acknowledged union activists with Dick considered the movement's most radical and militant voice. Laura was active but considered more moderate. She organized and served as the first president of the Aberdeen Women's Auxiliary.

Dick's extremism labeled him the designation as a Communist, placing him in fundamental disagreement with most of the local labor groups. The party had minimal influence within Aberdeen's union movement.

Despite philosophical differences, union leaders from all over Washington rallied around Law's cause and formed a defense team called the Grays Harbor Civil Rights

Committee. The group wanted to tie in Laura Law's murder into the local ransacking of the Finnish Workers Federation Hall just prior. They organized to expose a pattern of violence in Aberdeen that denied union activists their civil rights and freedom of expression. Law's flagrant murder was portrayed as an example.

Laura Law was born Lea Laura Luoma in Finland in 1914 and immigrated to the United States in 1920. Her father was an active union member having worked in the sawmills for several years. Laura was well-versed and passionate towards labor related issues. She found empathy with the grievances and dismal conditions for workers and families caught within the economic catastrophe of the Great Depression. The economic downturn severely impacted Aberdeen. The city had a very influential but divided Finnish community.

Local ethnic tensions inflamed with the December 1939 invasion of Finland by the Soviet Union. The conflict divided the union membership with the more militant minority factions, represented by Dick Law, supporting the Soviet invasion. The majority, consisting of anti-communists groups condemned the attack and raised money for relief efforts.

This turmoil resulted in the Finish Workers Federation Hall being ransacked by vigilantes opposing all Communist associations and radical policies. The mob's actions preceded Laura's death by a few weeks. The state of Washington has historically been at the center of several fatal union clashes throughout the first half of the twentieth century.

Investigators were never able to isolate a single suspect based on the evidence. Dick Law identified ten individuals who had sufficient motive for killing Laura. A noted Seattle detective was brought in by the local police department, but could not arrive at a conclusive result.

The murder remains unsolved. The modest house where Laura Law was slain has been subsequently razed. A vacant tract remains.

Finland would revenge the Soviet invasion with its own duplicity. Their leaders allowed Adolph Hitler's German forces to freely cross the country during their invasion of Russia amidst World War II. This blight of conscience for an evil but retributive act is often conveniently forgotten and rarely publicly discussed except amongst historians.

The antagonism between Russia and Finland remains profound. This hatred appears ironic when one considers that the Finnish national territory was once part of the Russian Empire until the conclusion of World War I.

Perhaps the Finns understood then and especially now very clearly the Russian leadership's mentality and ambitions. The western world often appears unable to grasp during previous periods of peaceful non-confrontation what seems so obvious to them.

**Laura Law Murder Site:
1117 East Second Street, Aberdeen**

Tom Wales: The Perfect Assassination?

At 10:40 p.m. on October 11, 2001, only one month following 9/11, Assistant United States Attorney Thomas Wales, 49, was sitting in front of his lighted home office computer located in his basement. Wales specialized in the investigation and prosecution of banking and business fraud.

An intruder entered his Seattle Queen Anne neighborhood driveway. He was cautious to avoid triggering the motion detector security lights in the backyard. A small ventilation window visibly exposed Wales. The intruder was armed with a rare former Soviet Bloc 9mm semi-automatic handgun. He fired four shots through the window into Wales's neck mortally wounding him. Wales managed to dial 911 before losing consciousness. Neighbors heard the shots. The killer fled either on foot or by vehicle discreetly leaving behind only shell casings.

The shooting resembled a professional hit with the exception of the scattered casings and the absence of a silencer. Given Wales' profession, the obvious question seemingly to determine motive was which of his cases and what prime suspect?

Wales had an unusual background with gun violence. At the Milton Academy prep school in Boston, he roomed with Joseph Patrick Kennedy, whose father Robert F. Kennedy was assassinated in 1968 at the Ambassador Hotel in Los Angeles. In 1995, a student at Garfield High, where Wales' son attended, brought a gun to school and shot two classmates.

Wales was a passionate gun-control advocate outside of his professional duties. His activism made him enemies. In

1997, he was the most visible and vocal supporter of an unsuccessful state referendum that would have required gun owners to use trigger locks.

A standing U.S. Department of Justice reward for one million dollars has turned up nothing substantial. The ante was upped to $1.52 million in 2018 with no substantive change. The National Association of Former United States Attorneys has established a matching fund. If the killing was indeed professionally committed, a suspect may never emerge. Wales, who had served in his capacity for eighteen years is presumed to be the only federal prosecutor ever killed in the line of duty.

The motive for his unprecedented killing was speculated to be retaliation for his work in a prior or ongoing investigation. The continued absence of substantive clues and leads sadly classifies the shooting as possibly a perfectly executed crime.

Tom Wales Murder Site:
108 Hayes Street, Seattle

A Manipulated Killing By A Simpleton

Clifford Cooper, 20 was a simpleton, easily manipulated and surrounded by acquaintances he perceived as friends.

He encountered Dan Lane through two former roommates, Velard and Cindy Saselli. Cooper and Lane shared mutual interests in hunting, trapping and guns. Cooper adored his pit bull *Scooter*. Lane introduced him into cocaine use. Over time he became Cooper's primary purchasing source. The relationship became strained when Lane bartered drugs instead of paying the cash amounts he'd offered for Cooper's personal possessions. Cooper did not like this arrangement, but failed to address his displeasure to him.

Velard *Joe* Saselli, 26 suspected that Lane was having an affair with his wife. On Tuesday, October 18, 1988, Cooper assisted the Sasellis move to a new residence. The following day, Joe Saselli informed Cooper of his plan to shoot Lane on Friday evening and asked him if he would drive him to the apartment while he committed the murder.

On Thursday evening, Saselli and Cooper began drinking together and the plan altered. Saselli urged the easily influenced Cooper to commit the murder instead because his bringing a gun inside Lane's house would be perceived as normal. He goaded Cooper repeatedly about Lane's manipulative behavior towards him. Cooper agreed to the change due to their friendship. Saselli stressed the need to kill any witnesses that might be present.

Nearing midnight Friday evening, Saselli drove Cooper to Lane's house. Cooper was dressed in jeans, tennis shoes, cap, a Halloween bald head and rubber gloves. Cindy Saselli had earlier applied women's make up on him probably unaware of his intentions. He wore a navy rain slicker over the outfit and carried his shotgun underneath his coat in a sling that he had purchased earlier that day.

When he arrived at Lane's house, he explained that he'd just returned from a Halloween party. As Lane turned away from him, Cooper lifted the shotgun and blasted him fatally three times. He also killed *Scooter* and wounded a guest, Patrick Fuquay with one shot.

Fuquay was still alive and conscious and asked Cooper why he had been shot. He then pleaded for his life. Cooper had emptied his remaining ammunition. He was aware of the location where Lane stored a pistol. He found the gun and approached Fuquay asking him to turn his head. He then unloaded seven shots into his skull.

During his subsequent confession, he indicated that he'd responded to Fuquay that *he didn't know why* that he had shot him. He rationalized that his second series of shots was *helping* Fuquay because he was *in so much pain*. Cooper picked up the visible 12-gauge shotgun shells and tossed them in bushes nearby as he exited.

The day following the murder, investigators questioned Cooper. He denied any involvement in the crime and indicated that he indeed owned a shotgun. When asked to exhibit the weapon, he escorted police to his truck and expressed astonishment that the gun was missing.

He would be arrested. During his 1999 trial, he would be sentenced to two consecutive life sentences plus additional years based on the cruel manner in executing Patrick Fuquay. Clifford remains interned the Monroe Correctional Complex. Saselli was charged with criminal assistance in the first-degree, but the results of his trial remained unpublished and his name is absent from the current Washington inmate search rolls.

**Dan Lane's Murder Site:
907 1/2 High Street, Bellingham**

Ann Marie Burr: A Mother's Torment of Never Knowing Her Daughter's Fate

It was a late Thursday evening on August 31, 1961 when the Burr family of Tacoma retired for the evening. Ann Marie Burr was the eldest daughter of four children. At the age of eight and a half, Ann slept with her younger sister in the upstairs bedroom. Her other two siblings slept in the basement inside a fortress they had constructed.

The mother, Beverly Burr chained and locked the front door, as was her custom. A fresh school year was approaching the following week. For parents like the Burrs, each succeeding school year acknowledged a fresh milestone in their children's growth.

Ann Marie Burr would not advance another school year. She would never be seen alive again. When the family awoke the next morning, she was gone.

In the course of the evening, an intruder leaned a bench underneath a side window. He slid open the window and crawled inside the house. Without disturbing anyone, he mounted the staircase and abducted Ann. He left only a partial palm print and a shoe print near his point of entry.

He and his victim vanished.

At the time, there were a few suspects. One was a high school neighbor boy and another a pair of itinerate Oregon bean pickers. All were questioned, but released for a lack of evidence.

Later the name of Ted Bundy would surface. The future serial killer, then 14, lived over three miles away, but reportedly knew Ann. He had a neighborhood paper route and one source indicated she followed him around habitually as he prepared his newspapers for delivery each afternoon.

Was the story factual and even credible? Was Anne Marie Burr his first victim?

Beverly Burr quizzed him via letters while he was incarcerated as to whether he was responsible for the kidnapping. He vehemently denied responsibility each time. The day before his execution, while he was confessing a litany of monstrous murders, he related a story about kidnapping a young girl and sexually assaulting her in an orchard next to her house. He indicated that after killing her, he laid her in a deep ditch and watched her parents and police anxiously search nearby.

An orchard existed adjacent to the Burr's house and ditches were plentiful that week during construction at nearby University of Puget Sound. Most of the deep holes had been paved over and filled with concrete within three days following the kidnapping.

Bundy was a known fabricator and enjoyed tormenting his accusers. He would have been intimately familiar with the kidnapping having been raised in Tacoma. Whether or not he actually knew Ann Marie or was ultimately responsible remains questionable, Beverly Burr was left in doubt. She passed away in 2008. Beverly endured every mother's nightmare concerning the safety and vulnerability of her children. Sadly, there was no closure as to the ultimate fate of her eldest daughter.

**Ann Marie Burr's Abduction Site:
3009 North 14th, Tacoma**

The Floating Fleet of Billy Ghol

Aberdeen has become most notably recognized as the birthplace of tragic Nirvana singer Kurt Cobain. It is a seaport harbor that he longed to escape and ultimately did through his music. The town built its reputation on shipping, lumber and inclimate weather.

The historic downtown features numerous remnants from its architectural past. The Crowther-Wooding Building on East Heron Street features the distinctive *Billy's Restaurant*, perhaps the sole establishment within the United States celebrating a deceased serial killer.

The interior showcases numerous nostalgic images from Aberdeen's past, particularly the Grays Harbor district. The proprietor is not named Billy. The namesake is in fact William Gohl, the former bartender at the Sailor's Union of the Pacific Building, further down the street. His former building is now a vacant lot adjacent to rotting pillars remaining from a distant era. Prior to Kurt Cobain, Billy Gohl was the city's most renowned celebrity.

Gohl arrived into Aberdeen via the Yukon and San Francisco. He quickly established his professional status as the official agent for the Sailor's Union. He was a stocky, steely-eyed brute that clearly demanded fear and respect. As the sole union representative and resident bartender, he was the initial contact for migrant sailors arriving into the port.

His role included acting as trustee for a visitor's incoming mail and funds. He would query incoming transients about their marital and family status. He was particularly keen on unattached men with financial means.

He earned a reputation for igniting labor strikes and uprisings. His violent temper and outbursts were legendary. Unknown to his patrons and associates, Billy had cultivated a secondary source of income, which reportedly he had begun during his prior city residences.

The unfortunate sailors that had confided in Gohl about their absence of family were often shot in the back or point blank in the head. Guhl's second floor office and bar featured a trash chute that stretched out into the Wishkah River below.

For seamen, bar brawls and their consequential homicides were not unusual and scarcely noted. During the course of 1909, excessive incidents of floating corpses led Aberdeen to be labeled as *The Port of Missing Men*. The cadavers became part of the *Floater Fleet*. Gohl initially escaped scrutiny for his role. He became one of the most vocal critics of the local law enforcement authorities for their inability to monitor and control the violence

Criminality laced by arrogance is often inseparable. In late December 1909, Gohl bragged to another saloon owner that he and a partner John Klingenburg would be killing two of his associates within 48 hours. The two perspective victims were shot, anchored and dumped into Aberdeen's waters. They were discovered a month later. Both Gohl and Klingenburg were arrested for the crime. Klingenberg provided a detailed confession implicating Gohl.

Billy Gohl was found guilty on two counts of murder. The revelations during his trial made him the prime suspect in an additional 41 deaths. Rumors suggested the actual total might have exceeded 150. The names of his victims remain anonymous.

He was sentenced on May 1910 to two consecutive life terms and initially served his time at the Washington State Penitentiary in Walla Walla. His turbulent prison stay prompted many violent attacks between inmates. A dementia from syphilis he had contracted during his waterfront years worsened.

He was transferred to the Sedro Woolley Mental Hospital and then in 1927, admitted to the State Hospital at Medical Lake in Spokane. He died on March 3, 1927 from pneumonia, erysipelas and demential paralytic at the age of 53.

Strange phenomena, paranormal occurrences and mischief have been reported at Billy's restaurant. Their source may be attributed to the wandering souls floating adrift the currents. Or, they may simply be the handiwork of a former malicious bartender who once haunted the town.

**Former Sailor's Union Hall Location (Above)
Billy's Bar and Grill, 322 E Heron Street, Aberdeen**

The Centralia Parade March and Massacre

Walking along the nearly deserted stretch of North Tower Street between West Second and West Third Streets in Centralia, there appears little reason to suspect anything of significance ever occurred. At one time, two hotels and a few notable commercial buildings lined the block. All have long since been demolished. Single-story unremarkable buildings include a liquor store, craft depot and an auto repair shop. The area feels far removed from the historic downtown center.

On November 11, 1919, this stretch between the two intersections was the site of an Armistice Day parade celebrating the conclusion of World War I. The event culminated in bloodshed between factions of participating American Legion brigades and the Industrial Workers of the World (IWW). Centralia and the neighboring town of Chehalis, participants in the parade, had large numbers of war veterans in both organizations.

Over a five-year period, animosities simmered and fermented between both sides. The IWW had philosophical affiliations with the communist movement in Russia. A successful revolution that had brought the Bolsheviks to power there was perceived as a potential threat to the democracies of Western Europe and the United States.

The next two decades became a period of fermenting international unrest erupting in a second global war. The leadership void during those years between would result in the ascension of dominant and aggressive political leaders such as Adolf Hitler (Germany), Joseph Stalin (Soviet Union), Benito Mussolini (Italy) and General Hideki Tojo (Japan).

In 1919, the cauldron was being stirred by conflicting influences. Centralia would serve as a microcosm. The IWW had attempted to obtain a union hall in 1917 employing an alias. Their landlord evicted them upon discerning their true identity. They succeeded in the spring of 1918, but the building was looted shortly afterwards during a local Red Cross parade. The IWW blamed hired thugs and members of the American Legion.

In 1919, the IWW reopened a union hall at the former Roderick Hotel on Tower Street near the intersection of Third Street. The union leadership vowed they would not be evicted again.

The November parade route encouraged a predictable disaster passing directly in front of the union hall and doubling back a second time. Armed conflict seemed inevitable. Centralia civic leaders, legion officers and union organizers delivered inflammatory speeches espousing their causes before the march. The rumor of confrontation prompted the local sheriff to decline to provide security services due to his scarce resources.

The menace heightened as an enthusiastic crowd swelled causing tight spacing and an unruly environment. Members of the American Legion marched with rubber hoses and gas pipes. Several members of the IWW were armed with high-powered rifles and stationed in front of buildings, on rooftops and nearby Seminary Hill along the route.

A stoppage of the procession resulted in the Chehalis continent of the American Legion pausing in front of the IWW union hall. The subsequent sequence of events would enflame Centralia.

As marchers waited, an IWW member Eugene Barnett, stationed atop the Avalon Hotel roof, fired an unobstructed shot at Legion Post Commander Warren Grimm. The bullet dropped Grimm where he stood and passed through his body. He was mortally wounded and dragged to the sidewalk. Legionnaire Arthur McElfresh, standing nearby, was hit in the brain with a .22 caliber shot fired from Seminary Hill over 500 yards away. He died instantly.

A fuselage rained down upon the vulnerable and unarmed Legionnaires. Amidst the melee and confusion, members stormed the Roderick Hotel and surrounding buildings.

This account at least was the American Legion's version of the story.

The IWW claimed that parade marchers from the American Legion during the delay, abruptly stormed the union hall with the intention of pillage as they had done the year previously at the Red Cross Parade festivities. They claimed their shots were fired in self-defense.

By the conclusion of the shootings, two additional legionnaires, Ben Cassagranda and Dale Hubbard were killed. Numerous participants were wounded and injured. Several members of the IWW contingent were arrested. One unfortunate detainee, Wesley Everest was snatched from prison by a vigilante mob the same evening. Mistaken for IWW leader Britt Smith, he was escorted to the Chehalis River Bridge and lynched.

In the days following the catastrophe, Centralia was isolated and governed by chaos. One resulting casualty four days later was Centralia Deputy Sheriff, John Haney. Members of a posse shot him to death because he failed to give a proper countersign.

The ensuing public trial in nearby Montesano brought charges against eleven apprehended members of the IWW. Mike Sheehan and Elmer Smith were acquitted, Loren Roberts was found not guilty by reason of insanity and six members, Eugene Barnett, Bert Bland, O.C. Bland, Ray Becker, John McInerney and John Lamb were convicted of second-degree murder. Bert Faulkner and Tom Morgan, who decided to turn state's evidence, had their charges dropped. Those convicted were sentenced to prison terms between 25-40 years. Two years later the group appealed the severity of their sentences to the Washington Supreme Court. The term lengths were re-affirmed by the court.

By 1930, citizen outrage cooled. A movement to release the Centralia Massacre prisoners gained momentum. Washington Governor Charles Martin commuted their sentences in 1933, but failed to overturn their convictions. The six, with the exception of Ray Becker were paroled. Becker maintained his innocence and refused several offers of parole without pardon. Finally in 1939, he was pardoned and released.

The extreme tragedy and irony behind the debacle was that each of the dead legionnaires had served their country with distinction in Europe during the calamity of the First World War.

It seems unimaginable that the bloody and violent incident that ended their lives could occur during an event celebrating victory. Yet it remains equally absurd that World War I, proclaimed *the war to end all wars* could be repeated within the span of a mere two decades with an even greater intensity of horror.

Centralia Massacre:

North Tower Street Between 2nd and 3rd Streets, Centralia

The Unsolved Kidnapping of Young Charles F. Mattson

As the financial agony of the Great Depression neared its first decade in 1936, an extreme means of crime emerged.

Kidnapping for ransom from the affluent received international headlines with the abduction and killing of Charles Lindbergh Jr. in March 1932. The convicted suspect Bruno Hauptmann, who maintained his innocence throughout his trial, was executed in 1936 following a controversial conviction.

On May 24, 1935, nine-year-old George Weyerhaeuser, the son of prominent lumber entrepreneur J. P. Weyerhaeuser was snatched on his way home from his Tacoma school. One week later, following extensive negotiations and a ransom payment, he was released in a shack near Issaquah. Three participants in the kidnapping scheme were captured. They were successfully tried and served extended prison sentences.

Young George Weyerhaeuser's kidnapping story had a fortunate ending. He would later become the Chairman of the Board for the Weyerhaeuser Company.

For ten-year-old Charles F. Mattson, the scenario ended differently.

On Sunday evening, December 27, 1936, Mattson was kidnapped from his living room by an armed masked man, a mere two blocks away from the Weyerhaeuser Mansion. The kidnapper targeted Charles who was playing with his older brother Billy, sister Muriel and her friend from Seattle, Virginia Chatsfield.

The Mattson parents were away at a social function and

returned home soon afterwards. A ransom note was left demanding $28,000.

Seventy pound Charles was carried away into the winter evening across the backyard and down a steep embankment towards Commencement Bay. His teenage siblings were mindful enough to telephone the police. The kidnapper's mask had fallen off amidst the escape enabling an eyewitness description by each of those present. It was presumed that he drove away via a nearby parked getaway car as a police search of the surrounding area and waters revealed nothing.

Over the course of the next two weeks, the case drew national attention. His father, William Mattson, a Tacoma physician and surgeon, made multiple attempts to pay the ransom. He reportedly had three direct communications by mail and telephone with the kidnapper. His efforts proved in vain.

On January 11, 1937, a hunter found the boy's battered body in a Snohomish County field near Everett. An examination of the remains indicated that Charles Mattson had been bound tightly with rope. He had suffered massive head injuries from beatings and appeared to have been stabbed in the back with a long-bladed knife.

It was speculated that his killing might have been the very evening of the abduction. Below freezing temperatures during the following week kept the body from decomposing. The conditions made it impossible to determine the actual time of death. President Franklin Roosevelt issued an official statement to the nation on the morning following the body's discovery.

Despite a substantive investigation by the FBI resulting in

interviews with approximately 26,000 people, no one was ever arrested and charged. Numerous eccentrics confessed, but usually to gain attention or due to mental illness.

The mystery behind Charles Mattson's kidnapping would ultimately baffle police and remain a tragic narrative in Tacoma's history. The stately Tudor-style Mattson Mansion would be unceremoniously razed in 2006 and rebuilt as a more contemporary sprawling complex.

The memory of young Charles Mattson's violent adduction and untimely killing seem incongruous with the serene panorama. The view from neighboring Point Defiance, which includes Commencement Bay and the Tacoma Narrows Bridge, remains breathtaking.

The kidnapping sadly reflected the desperation of an era plagued by financial catastrophe.

Charles Mattson Kidnapping Site
4605 N. Verde Street, Tacoma

**Weyerhaeuser Mansion
4301 North Stevens Street**

Chief Leschi's Execution: A Legacy of Shame

The legacy of abuse initiated by the United States Government towards the Native American tribes has been documented extensively.

One of the most prominent and respected Pacific Northwest names during the mid-nineteenth century was Chief Leschi. He was born in 1808 to mixed tribal parentage. His father was Nisqually and mother Yakama. He was appointed chief by Washington's first territorial governor, Isaac Stevens to represent the Nisqually and Puyallup tribes. On December 26, 1854, he was obliged to sign a treaty, which transferred Indian lands to the United States government. His tribe was coerced into inhabiting inferior reservation territory.

Leschi signed the unfavorable post-Christmas treaty with an "X" either out of protest or illiteracy. His mark may have also been forged. His tribe was relocated to a rocky piece of high ground unsuitable for growing food. They were completely severed from access to a river that had traditionally provided their mainstay livelihood of salmon.

In 1855, Leschi traveled to the territorial capital in Olympia to protest the treaty terms. Acting Governor Charles Mason ordered that Leschi and his brother, Quiemuth be taken into *protective* custody by force en route. Upon the order, Leschi led a small contingent of 300 warriors and engaged in small skirmishes around the periphery of the settlements. Two militiamen, Abram Benton Moses and Joseph Miles were killed in the fighting.

Leschi and his party were deemed responsible for the killings. Martial law was declared in the region. For a year, he remained a fugitive. Leschi was captured in November

1856 and his brother was forced to turn himself in shortly afterwards. An unknown assailant murdered Quiemuth within a week.

In 1858, Chief Leschi was charged for killing Abram Moses, but the trial resulted in a hung jury. The results were based on the judge's instructions that the killing of combatants during wartime did not constitute murder. In his second trial, the judge did not provide similar instructions and Leschi was convicted and sentenced to death. He denied being the responsible party throughout the proceedings. His attorneys were not allowed to present evidence.

Not everyone was convinced of his guilt. Amongst his proponents included several newspaper writers and Pierce County Sheriff, George Williams. The sheriff allowed himself to be arrested for insubordination rather than carry out the execution.

Leschi was hastily hung in a small valley on a quickly constructed gallows near Lake Stellacoom. His hangman protested the travesty but carried out his duty. The site reportedly later became a golf course and then a housing development.

Leschi and his unjust treatment have not been entirely forgotten. In the late 1880's, a central Seattle neighborhood was named after him. It remains one of the most volatile in the city. Numerous streets, parks and monuments bear his name.

In 2004, the Washington state legislature symbolically passed a resolution exonerating him. The gesture, although well intentioned, proved 146 years too late to cleanse the stain and consequence of a historical travesty. Leschi's death would simply be another example amongst an era of shameful national theft.

**19th Century Olympia Jailhouse Location
Legion and Adams Street, Olympia**

Fred Ross Ring Death: The Inherent Dangers of Exhibition Fighting

A 20-round boxing exhibition between Fred *Iron Man* Ross from Colorado and Jack Donnelly from Montana was the highlight of the Aberdeen Fourth of July festivities in 1905. The match was preceded by a local parade and a baseball contest between the local amateur squad and neighboring Hoquiam team at the Electric Park ballfield.

Following the game, a temporary boxing ring was set up. Reserved seating was in the grandstands with general admission in the bleachers. The lightweight division match was billed as a 20-round exhibition. Typically an unsanctioned bout like this featured predominantly sparring only with the combatants splitting the gate receipts.

For the first fifteen rounds, both fighters bobbed, weaved and occasionally struck each other. The only damage inflicted was to their endurance as both became fatigued. Locked in a clench, Donnelly shoved Ross away towards the mat. Due to their entanglement, he followed and landed upon the other fighter. Ross' head struck the ring mat, which was unpadded. Most states required padding but Washington law did not. Fighters preferred the stiffer surface as it aided in the speed of their footwork.

Donnelly rose immediately from the pile, ready to resume fighting. Ross remained prone and unconscious. He remained immobile. A ringside doctor present attended to him immediately. He was driven to the Aberdeen General Hospital, but expired that night shortly around midnight.

The cause of death was determined to be a blood clot at the base of his brain resulting from the concussion of his head striking the mat.

The following day, Jack Donnelly was charged with manslaughter. At his preliminary hearing, the judge ruled that the criteria for a homicide were not present. Both parties were aware of the inherent risks involved with the match. He ruled the death *accidental* and acquitted Donnelly of all charges. Donnelly would continue fighting until 1911 securing two additional draws and ending his career with an official record of zero wins, three losses and four draws. Ross' funeral was sparsely attended with no family members present.

Over the following decade, Seattle, Tacoma, Spokane and several Washington cities would ban prize fighting within their city limits. The prohibitions in most instances would last over two decades. The reasons cited included the violence, gambling and unsavory attendees the matches attracted.

Electric Park has since been dismantled. It became ironically the location for the Aberdeen Public Utilities large equipment and salvage yard. No memorials regarding the former stadium or infamous boxing match are evident.

On April 2015, at Aberdeen's *Brawl at the Mall*, an amateur mixed-martial arts fight card, Jameston Lee-Yaw, 47 collapsed in the changing room following the completion of his bout. He was given CPR and then hospitalized. He died two days later. None of his training crew suspected anything unusual during or immediately afterwards. His death was ruled due to kidney failure. His brother did not attribute his death as a result of the fight. Fight promoters were expedient to post on social media that the cause was a *pre-existing condition*.

Boxing and now mixed martial arts fighting remain

dangerous occupations. The prize money is substantial at the highest levels. For the majority of men and women who actively participate, the risks are apparent. Society has yet to find an adequate reason for abolishing ring violence.

Spectator enthusiasm, television viewership and the acclaim earned by fighters guarantee that physical combat will continue to remain popular spectacles.

**Fred Ross Boxing Death:
Electric Park Aberdeen, 2720 Sumner Avenue (Now Gray's Harbor PUD Large Equipment and Salvage Yard)**

Everett Dockside Massacre: Sunday Bloody Sunday

The term *Bloody Sunday* is commonly referred to the *troubles* in Northern Ireland that accelerated when British soldiers opened fire on unarmed and fleeing protestors in Derry in 1972. Fourteen people died and the violence stimulated a consolidating recruitment tool for the Irish Republic Army in their struggle for separation from British rule.

The conflict seethed and raged for the next three successive decades before various treaties and agreements stilled the fighting between England and Protestant and Catholic separatist factions. The absence of casualty grabbing headlines has not permanently ceased the resentment.

During the early twentieth century, the Pacific Northwest was a vortex of conflict between union organizations and commercial interests. Unions and politics were inseparable. Movements that have resisted authority have often attracted violence.

As with the cities of Centralia and Seattle, armed conflicts and union strikes characterized the particularly unstable environment between 1916-1920, as global war raged.

On November 5, 1916, Everett became a lethal skirmish amongst extended labor unrest. The city was in the midst of an economic depression. Violence had erupted on numerous occasions fueled by rallies and street orators. Local law enforcement was resolutely aligned with commercial interests and business owners.

A violent showdown on the city docks became an inevitable flashpoint. The armed confrontation occurred on a Sunday, historically the sole day of leisure from the grinding demands of commerce.

The most prominent union, the Industrial Workers of the World (IWW) had galvanized a team of 300 supporters to join the embattled workforce of Everett. Local shingle workers were in the midst of a five-month strike that showed little promise of resolution. The contingent boarded two Seattle based passenger ferries and headed for the Everett port.

Local authorities had anticipated their arrival in the early afternoon. Armed vigilantes, deputized citizens, hostile hired thugs and law enforcement authorities awaited their docking. Their greeting was absent of welcome. As one of the ships, the *Verona* entered the dock area and threw a line over a bollard, Everett Sheriff Donald McRae called out: *Boys, who's your leader?*

The union members and sympathizers on board jeered and laughed. They replied *We're all leaders*!

The sheriff identified himself and asserted his authority. He withdrew his pistol and informed the group they could not land at the port. Ignoring his menace, a gangplank was stretched out. It never reached shore. The boat never landed in Everett.

There was silence as both parties surveyed the other.

A single shot rang out followed by approximately ten minutes of intense gunfire. Innocent passengers were interspersed with the IWW members and many rushed to the opposite end of the boat nearly capsizing it. The ship's rails broke and passengers were ejected into the waters. Some drowned. It was estimated over 175 bullets pierced the pilothouse alone and the captain, Chance Wiman narrowly escaped death by ducking behind the ship's safe.

The ship's engineer and captain were able to re-direct the steamer away from a worse catastrophe. They navigated the vessel back to Seattle and warned the incoming second boat to reverse course away from Everett.

At the conclusion of the carnage, a fixed casualty rate became impossible to determine. Two citizen deputies lay dead from *friendly* fire and between 7-12 IWW members were estimated to be killed. The wounded exceeded 50. Ironically after the gunfire exchange, the Everett IWW began a street rally that resulted in numerous arrests. Washington's governor sent companies of militia to both Everett and Seattle to assist in maintaining order.

Upon the *Verona's* return to Seattle, 75 members of the IWW including their leader Thomas Tracy were arrested for the murder of the two deputies. Following a two-month trial in May 1917, Tracy was acquitted and the remaining defendants released from jail.

Today the historic Everest dockside pillars emerge from the waters blunted and splintered from disuse and neglect. The commute between Seattle and Everett is conducted by freeway.

Conflicting versions attributing guilt have emerged including the interspersing of paid instigators by the business owners within the ranks of union orators. The truth and fixed blame may be more accurately assigned to the extremes between the *haves* and *have-nots* of the era. The contemporary gap between wealth and poverty have only widened with time.

Economics ultimately fuel revolution and war. The warring class struggles leave casualties. It is difficult to imagine a day when this condition will no longer be a constant.

Former site of Everett's ferry docks and massacre

Sylvia Gaines: The Final Vestiges of Scandal Has Been Removed

The final reminder of an unsettling murder that shocked Seattle was felled in 1999 when the Park Department determined that 30 large black cottonwood trees posed a public safety threat due to their falling limbs. The trees had been planted in 1929 at Gaines Point on the north end of Green Lake Park. Gaines Point was named after 22-year-old Sylvia Gaines, whose dead body was discovered in an alder tree grove there.

On the early morning of June 17, 1926, Gaines' shoes were found by a carpenter strolling along the lake en route to work. A few yards further was Gaines' body, nearly naked and sprawled near the shore.

The news of the murder initially transfixed Seattle and the repugnant revelations that would emerge following her death kept the story newsworthy. The prime suspect was her father, Bob Gaines, a World War I veteran and the brother of William Gaines, the chairman of the King County Board of Commissioners.

Bob Gaines had migrated to Seattle from Massachusetts in 1909 following the break-up of his marriage. Sylvia, his only daughter from the marriage was born in 1904 and scarcely knew her father, having last seen him when she was five. Following her graduation from Smith College in 1925, she arrived for a September visit.

The paternal bond proved far from traditional. Rumors began almost immediately upon her arrival. Her father lived in a diminutive one-bedroom house. He and his second wife slept together in the bedroom and Sylvia on the couch...at least initially. The threesome quarreled regularly and the living arrangements shifted.

Mrs. Gaines reportedly tried to kill herself in November. Reports of indiscreet exchanges between father and daughter in Woodland Park and in a downtown Seattle hotel were introduced at his murder trial. It became assumed that they had consummated an incestuous sexual relationship. It was further rumored that they were planning to move in together in an apartment.

The unseemly arrangement apparently exhausted its novelty when Sylvia became fed up with the tension in the household. She planned to leave and move in with her uncle William Gaines. The fallout from her departure was apparent. She might have been inclined towards revealing the incestuous affair to her uncle.

On June 16, at approximately 8 p.m., Bob Gaines became inebriated, violent and argued bitterly with his daughter. She left the house to get away from him. He tracked and followed her still enraged. At his trial, the prosecutor indicated that he caught up with her an hour later. Sylvia was strangled and beaten with a rock, which was located nearby, coated in her blood.

Forensics indicated that her body had been dragged several yards from the murder spot and arranged in a manner to suggest a sexual assault.

Witnesses indicated seeing Gaines bending over something or someone in the vicinity at that hour. Other witnesses spotted him driving around the lake several times preceding the murder. The most damaging testimony came from his best friend, Louis Stern. Gaines arrived at his house to continue his drinking binge at 9:30 p.m. His comments to Stern resembled a confession.

At his trial, the jury deliberated scarcely over three hours, before finding him guilty of murder and sentenced him to death. He appealed the sentence, but was unsuccessful. On August 31, 1928, Bob Gaines was hung at the State Penitentiary in Walla Walla. His body was interned at the Evergreen-Washelli Memorial Park with full military honors. Sylvia was cremated and her ashes sent to her mother in South Lynfield, Massachusetts.

Gaines Point is a distant memory to most daily strollers along Green Lake. The alder and replacement cottonwood trees are gone. They have been replaced by an indistinguishable poplar grove resembling the majority that lines the lakeside.

The taint behind the Gaines scandal long ago disappeared. With the eternal frailty of the human condition, screaming headlines have merely shifted to a fresh new drama.

**Sylvia Gaines Murder Site:
Gains Point (near Meridian Street intersection), Green
Lake Park located along Green Lake Drive, Seattle**

West Seattle Bridge: A Collision With An Unanticipated Destiny

What voters and elected officials could not accomplish through the customary legislative channels, an errantly steered freighter did. The original low-level West Seattle Bridge was constructed in 1924, but created horrendous traffic jams due to frequent bridge openings necessitated by Duwamish Waterway ship traffic.

On June 11, 1978, the freighter *Antonio Chavez* struck the original bascule bridge while passing underneath. No one was injured. The collision left the bridge stuck open and beyond temporary repair. It was declared inoperable.

The collision enabled a convenient solution to an ongoing chronic problem. Concerted replacement efforts had been initiated nearly twenty years before. A local ballot measure was passed in 1968 and other funding sources allocated towards the project.

During the reconstruction competitive bidding process, a major bribery scandal was uncovered involving the Head of Washington's House Transportation Committee. The aftermath, following the trials and imprisonment of conspirators, resulted in the legislature withdrawing designated monies towards the project. The 1978 collision proved timely qualifying access to federal repair funds for the bridge's reconstruction.

In 1984, a replacement span officially called the *Jeanette Williams Memorial Bridge* was opened reconnecting West Seattle with the rest of the city.

The cantilevered segmental design spans the east and west channels that form the mouth of the Duwamish River as it enters Elliott Bay and crosses over Harbor Island. The 2,600-foot long bridge's main approaches are Fauntleroy Way S.W. from the west and the Spokane Street Viaduct from the east. Average daily traffic is 137,400 vehicles.

The captain of the unfortunate freighter, Rolf Neslund was forced into retirement at the age of eighty-one because of the accident. It was rumored that he had a drinking problem and was considered *too old* to be piloting freighters. The pragmatic Neslund feared he would lose his assets due to potential lawsuits and transferred his entire pension monies to his wife Ruth, twenty-three years younger.

Much to his alarm and chagrin, Ruth spent the entirety within two years. They quarreled violently. Ruth ended the conflict on August 8, 1980 by shooting him to death twice in the head.

With the assistance of her older brother, she chopped up his body with a butcher knife and ax, incinerating the pieces in a barrel and dumping the ashes in a pile of manure behind their Lopez Island home.

The major flaw in her strategy was despite his drinking issues, Rolf had friends and colleagues that missed him. They prompted a missing-persons investigation by the San Juan County Sheriff's Department. Without a *body* for evidence but a certain motive, the Sheriff's department charged Ruth Neslund with first-degree murder. She was found guilty in 1985 and sentenced to life in prison. She died incarcerated of natural causes eight years later.

The West Seattle Bridge today offers sufficient shipping clearance. Despite the normally fluid flow, increasing traffic loads have made the rush hour commute an increasingly unwelcome nightmare.

The bridge was closed in March 2020 after cracks in the underside were found to be growing rapidly, necessitating major repairs. Target date for reopening is mid-2022.

**West Seattle Bridge Collision:
Base of Jeanette Williams Memorial Bridge spanning the Duwamish Waterway**

Murderous Revenge Spawned By The *Brides of Christ* Cult

Five days following his May 2, 1906 arrival from Portland, Oregon, George Mitchell sighted his prey. The mill worker wasted minimal time fulfilling the object of his visit.

Franz Edmund Creffield and his wife Maud were strolling leisurely down Seattle's First Avenue that day completely unaware of Mitchell's identity or lurking shadow. Mitchell posed leisurely in front of the Quick Drugstore at the intersection of Cherry Street. As the couple passed, he raised a 32-calibre revolver to the back of Creffield's neck and fired a single shot.

Creffield died instantly as did a religious movement that he had founded three years earlier in Corvallis, Oregon. He was previously a Salvation Army worker. After renaming himself Joshua, he founded his cult rejecting materialism, assuming that someone else provided him sustenance.

The group began their services on Kilger Island (on the periphery of Corvallis), then and now rural farming grounds laden with water bodies and numerous trees to camouflage their activities from curious prying eyes.

The majority of his twenty members were women who liberally incinerated their clothing, corsets and hats as sacramental rites. They wore wrappers that were long shapeless tunics. Locals labeled his adherents *Holy Rollers* due to their orgasmic rolling on the ground during religious services. The church's adopted name was the *Brides of Christ*.

Members lived communally, marriage was eschewed and Creffield indulged his sexual appetite on many of the members. The cult was tossed from their initial benefactor's home when they ignited a bonfire of his family's possessions in front of his house. Speculation abounded that household pets had been tossed into the flames heightening fears that human sacrifices might follow. Creffield became the lover of his benefactor's wife and daughter.

Alarmed male residents of Corvallis banded together on the evening of January 4, 1904 to tar and feather Creffield. The following morning, he revenged the act by marrying his former host's daughter Maud. He prudently skipped town before a follow-up vigilante band could return that evening with a hanging rope.

Creffield had temporarily evaded Corvallis, but remained in Oregon. A few months later an adultery criminal complaint was lodged against him in Portland stating that he had engaged in sexual relations with a married devotee as part of a purification ritual.

The local press speculated that she was merely one of fifteen women that Creffield had seduced or violated. Some of these women were transferred to the Salem insane asylum and the younger ones to the Oregon Girls' Aid Society. George Mitchell's 15-year old sister Esther was one of these young women.

Creffield went into hiding to avoid capture. Lacking financial resources, he opted to hide under the porch of his former benefactor. During that period, he became bearded, filthy, nearly starving and naked. He was slipped food and water clandestinely by some of his devotees including the wife and daughter of his former host.

Discovered and then arrested, Creffield was convicted of

adultery at his trial and sentenced to state prison for two years. While incarcerated for seventeen months, prophet Creffield changed his name to Elijah. He hatched a new strategy to reorganize and summoned several of his former followers to gather in Waldport, Oregon. The costal village would become temporarily his new Eden. Several women trekked on foot to join him.

Basking in newfound confidence and redemption, Franz Edmund Creffield reportedly cursed the *Sodoms* of Seattle, Portland, Corvallis and San Francisco. A few days later, a devastating earthquake and fire nearly destroyed San Francisco.

Creffield migrated north with his wife to Seattle. When George Mitchell learned of his whereabouts, he pursued by train. Following the murder, he surrendered to police without resistance. The cult's former benefactor and primary victim provided him with top legal representation. He pled *temporary insanity*. At trial, his defense team vilified the indefensible Creffield. Witnesses portrayed him unceasingly as a *reptile* and *human vampire*.

The jury quickly exonerated Mitchell. His father, brothers and male Corvallis residents celebrated his act of reclaiming the honor of his sister. The gesture however was unappreciated by the intended beneficiary and Creffield's wife. Esther Mitchell met her brother at Seattle's King Street station as the Mitchell family was preparing to board a return train to Portland. As a consolatory act, she shook his hand in front of the assemblage. As he prepared to board the train, she raised a pistol hidden under a coat draped over her arm. She fired one shot in the exact same spot on his neck that had killed Creffield. The bullet severed an artery and he bled to death on the station platform.

Esther Mitchell and Maud Creffield expressed no remorse at their trial. Creffield freely admitted that she had purchased the gun and ammunition following George Mitchell's acquittal. Both women were declared delusional and dangerous. Maud Creffield was deported to the Oregon state insane asylum. She managed to have strychnine smuggled into the county jail cell during her appeal process and committed suicide.

Esther Mitchell spent two years at the Western State Hospital in Steilacoom before being declared *cured*. In 1914 at the age of 26, she relocated to Waldport, Oregon. Externally happy, she ended her life as well with strychnine only three months into a recent marriage.

In 1975, Marshall Applewhite and Bonnie Nettles staged a recruiting session at a Waldport motel that was heavily attended for their newly founded Heaven's Gate cult. During March 19-20, 1997, thirty-nine members of the group including Applewhite ingested a lethal mixture of phenobarbital diluted with applesauce and vodka. Their mass suicide coincided with the Comet Hale-Bopp orbiting near the earth.

**George Mitchell's Assassination of Franz Creffield:
Former Quick Drugstore location
Corner of First Avenue and Cherry Street, Seattle**

**Esther Mitchell's Shooting location of Brother George:
King Street Station Portland Bound Platform
303 South Jackson Street, Seattle**

People's Theatre: The Legacy of Seattle's Private Female Performers and Police Chief Killer

The Schlesinger-Brodek Block Building was constructed in 1890 upon the ashes of the Great Fire. Original owners John Schlesinger and Gustav Brodek at some point, transferred title to Robert Abrams. He then leased the structure to Captain James Nugent and the basement to future theatre impresario John Considine.

Considine operated the *People's Theatre* between 1891-1894 and again in 1898-1910 between local anti-vice campaigns. The theatre was known for magic acts, singing, dancing, minstrel shows, but more prominently for lewd acts and actresses selling their sexual services within cloistered dark booths. The *People's box house* became infamous. Concurrently, it also served as a launching point for quality local professional entertainment.

John Considine was an individual of extreme contradictions. Raised through the Chicago parochial school system, he was briefly a policeman before departing the region as an itinerate stage actor. He dealt cards, but never played. He earned significant proceeds from peddling alcohol and sex but didn't drink and was known as a devoted family man.

His rise to local prominence resulted in a monopoly of three gaming houses and a cooperative relationship with Police Chief C. S. Reed. One of his noteworthy era competitors was legendary Wyatt Earp. Considine unsuccessfully attempted to intimidate Earp when he opened a flourishing competing operation. The state of Washington ultimately succeeding in thwarting Earp's ambitions. They filed criminal charges against him, confiscated and then burned the establishment's furnishings.

Considine's good fortune and monopoly waned when William L. Meredith, a former employee, was hired as Seattle's Police Chief. Their former relationship and allegiance soured. Meredith began exclusively targeting Considine's operations with arrests, fines and harassment under the guise of a crackdown campaign. Competitors operated unmolested provided payoffs were timely deposited. The schism between both men evolved into legal antagonism. Considine accused Meredith of flagrant corruption and the police chief's job status became vulnerable resulting in his forced resignation, Meredith accused Considine of impregnating one of his performers, a 17-year-old contortionist.

Their animosity took an abruptly violent turn when on June 25, 1901 a heavily armed Meredith stalked Considine (who was carrying two guns) in front of the H. K. Owen Building. The building was then owned by Henry Yesler and known as G. O. Guy's drugstore. Meredith took direct aim at Considine with a sawed-off shotgun, fired and somehow missed. Considine was stunned and took refuge in the drugstore. Meredith pursued. He fired again nearly wounding two others and clipped Considine in the back of the neck. Wounded superficially, Considine managed to disable Meredith with a bear hug. He dragged him towards the entrance, yelling for assistance from his brother Tom, standing nearby.

Tom grabbed one of his brother's two pistols and smashed the grip over Meredith's skull. He then fended off arriving policemen with the drawn weapon. John Considine pointed his second weapon at Meredith, who was still moving and reaching for another firearm in his arsenal. He finished Meredith off with three shots to the chest and neck. He then surrendered the gun and himself to arriving Seattle Sheriff Cudihee.

At the sensational public trial, the jury acquitted Considine within three hours of deliberation based on his self-defense claim. Meredith had been overheard making boasting statements about killing Considine less than 24-hours prior to their confrontation.

Afterwards, Considine did not discreetly exit the Seattle stage. Instead, he reinvented himself and changed neighborhoods. In 1902, he acquired Seattle's first movie theatre, the Edison's Unique Theatre, partnering with the local distributor of Edison phonograph records. Seattle's distance from other West Coast urban populations resulted in Considine's establishment of a Pacific Northwestern vaudeville circuits extending north into British Columbia. His pathway towards respectability included co-founding the Fraternal Order of Eagles and the expansion of a nationwide vaudeville circuit in conjunction with *Big Tim* Sullivan, a New York City Tammany Hall boss.

Considine's professional rivalry with another Seattle-based theatre promoter, Alexander Pantages eventually shuttered his local operations. Booking talent became scarce during the World War I years and his circuit fell apart. Pantages acquired the remnants. Both men eventually relocated to Los Angeles and became fixtures in the developing film industry. Considine's legacy and stature has been reinforced by the success of his film producer son, John Jr. and grandsons, film and television actors John and Tim Considine.

Above the *People's Theatre* basement, the original three-story Queen Anne and Richardsonian Romanesque design remains despite the loss of its upper two floors during the

1949 Earthquake. Building facades face Washington Street and the Second Avenue South Extension. Its stunted design and detailing remain essential gridded Victorian composition with the employment of brick corbelling.

Following the *People's Theatre* demise, William *Billy* Belond opened a tavern in the basement called *Billy Mug's*, noteworthy for a 50-foot-long bar and the accurate drink sliding skills of his employed bartenders. Later, an after hours venue opened known officially as *The Casino* and informally as *Madame Peabody's Dancing Academy for Young Ladies*.

Above ground, in 1934, Seattle's (and possibly America's) first openly gay bar, the *Double Header* opened on the Second Avenue façade. The bar closed at the end of 2015. Next door sharing the building, Barney's Jewelry and Loan has operated as a pawnshop for decades.

**Schlestiner-Brodek, Nugent and Considine Block Building, People's Theatre
172 Washington Street South, Seattle**

**G. O. Guy's Drugstore:
Corner Second Avenue at Yester Way, Seattle**

David Lee Childs: An Aesthetic Violated By Vulgarity

Fetish or fascination? David Lee Childs, 70, shared an obsession towards shoes dating back to the 1960s. A lifetime resident of Yakima, he retired after 31 years of selling shoes at the local Nordstrom's department store. During his adult life, he had amassed a distinctive collection of over 600 pairs, which he had displayed at the Yakima Valley Museum during a two-year exhibition.

Inoffensive and well regarded, Childs seemed the least likely person one would discover fatally beaten and stabbed 38 times in a concrete flower planter in downtown Yakima. His March 18, 2013 killing proved so severe, investigators required several days to accurately identify the body. Eventually his name was found inscribed under a set of false teeth he was wearing.

Police were utterly baffled as to a motive against a man genuinely liked and respected. Their wait was brief.

A witness came forward the morning after Childs' body was discovered with a photograph he had taken the night before around 11 p.m. The shot portrayed a man standing over another who was lying on the ground. The photo showed both the man and a vehicle next to him.

The car license plate was traced was traced to nearby Wapato and the residence of 34 year old Armando Vieyra. Officers found Vieyra home and a match to the individual in the photograph, He was taken into custody.

In media accounts, Vieyra acknowledged encountering Childs the evening of the murder at the Yakima Arcade. The two apparently engaged in sexual activity. Vieyra claimed he pushed Childs to the ground after some unwanted touching, but denied injuring or killing him. His explanation was ridiculed by the Yakima Police Chief based on the brutality inflicted by 38 stab wounds.

At trial, Vieyra pleaded guilty to second-degree murder and was sentenced to 14 years in prison. He is currently incarcerated at the Coyote Ridge Corrections Center following initial internment at Washington State Penitentiary in Walla Walla. The fate and location of David Lee Child's shoe collection has not been revealed.

**David Lee Childs Murder Site:
N Front Street & Yakima Avenue Flower Bed, Yakima**

Delbert Belton: The Savage Beating of an Elderly World War II Veteran

Like many of his generation, 88-year-old Delbert Belton enthusiastically enlisted in the United States military during World War II. He fought with distinction in the battle of Okinawa despite sustaining a bullet wound in his leg.

He returned to Spokane after the conflict and spent decades working at Kaiser Aluminum before retiring. Much of his subsequent retirement time was spent at the Eagles Fraternal Lodge playing pool, working on cars and socializing. The diminutive Delbert was affectionately nicknamed *Shorty* and well liked.

Demetrius Glenn and Kenan Adams-Kinard, both 16, randomly targeted Belton on the evening of August 22, 2013 while he sat in his car in the Eagle's parking lot waiting for a friend. The pair robbed and ruthlessly beat him, leaving Belton to die. He succumbed to his injuries shortly after being taken to a hospital.

Glenn turned himself in to police shortly after investigators distributed surveillance photos. Police discovered Adams-Kinard a few days later, cowering in an apartment. He had the audacity to claim the vicious beating was the result of an aborted crack cocaine deal where Belton had shorted him. Police immediately dismissed his absurd explanation.

Court documents indicated that the Aryan Brotherhood, a white supremacist group, had put a $10,000 bounty on the lives of the two suspects. Both were temporarily relocated into adult facilities due to safety concerns.

At his January 2015 trial, Kenan Adams-Kinard pleaded guilty to first-degree murder charges in exchange for two lesser charges being dropped. He was sentenced to 20 years in prison. He is currently incarcerated at the Washington State Penitentiary. Demetrius Glenn, during his later trial, also pleaded guilty and was sentenced to 16 years. He is currently imprisoned at the Coyote Ridge Corrections Center.

Outrage over the senseless death stunned and prompted members of the Spokane community to create makeshift memorials acknowledging Belton's contribution to society. For one who served valiantly to preserve global freedom during his youth, the audacity of preying on his later frailty becomes particularly odious.

**Delbert Belton's Murder Site:
Eagle's Lodge, 6410 North Ligerwood Street, Spokane**

John Anthony Castro: A Careless and Violent Lifestyle with Predictable Consequences

Spokane seems a universe away from the fame and riches of rap music industry superstardom. For an aspiring act such as John Anthony Castro who titled himself *Lil Danger*, the distance became insurmountable with a single impulsively fired gunshot.

Jose Solis, Jr. was part of a rival rap group from Moses Lake that was attending a concert in a Spokane downtown sushi bar on November 27, 2011. He shared similar musical ambitions as Castro. Solis and his companions had rented a block of rooms at the downtown Quality Inn on the fourth floor.

During the course of the evening, their group had encountered Castro and some of his associates. Words were exchanged at the concert venue and the conflict spilled over to the hotel into the early morning hours. Solis, 21, attempted to intervene in a fight between factions and was shot in chest by Castro from a distance of six to eight feet.

Police arrived at the hotel at approximately 2:32 a.m. as friends were attempting to transport Solis out of the hotel via an elevator. Their efforts were in vain as he was pronounced dead at a local hospital.

Castro fled immediately but a member of Solis' party followed him and memorized the license plate of his vehicle. Another friend had photographed the getaway car with her cell phone. Castro was arrested soon afterwards running from a downtown traffic stop.

Castro was familiar to trouble. His criminal history began in 1996 and included nine felony convictions. His two prior violent convictions qualified him for mandatory life in prison without parole. His messy lifestyle included fathering three children. His girlfriend at the time was pregnant.

Lil Danger was a small-scale regional performer with a pair of self-produced albums. He described himself on social media websites as a tour participant with the *Planet of the Apes* concert series covering the Pacific Northwest during the summer of 2011.

One of his two album covers features an ominous dark background with Castro sitting between two skeletons in a burial crypt. In front of him on a table are a pistol with stacks of currency, a marijuana baggie and several bricks of cocaine. Another cover features Castro in front of a message board pointing a stick towards contemporary gang terminology references. Both albums mirror the iconic clichés and redundant themes the rap music industry has sadly come to personify.

At his 2013 trial, Castro was convicted of second-degree murder, felony riot and unlawful possession of a firearm. The courtroom was packed with friends and family of both Castro and Solis creating the potential for further violence. Castro was sentenced to life imprisonment where he is currently serving his term at the Coyote Ridge Corrections Center following a stint at the State Penitentiary in Walla Walla. With the announcement of the verdict, sheriff deputies were obliged to segregate and escort each group separately out of the building. They stood guard at the courthouse until both contingents had completely left peaceably.

Castro's future parole eligibility will ultimately be argued and appealed before a judge over the next subsequent years.

However, it is safe to conclude that whatever talent or promise Castro exhibited as a musician was squandered by his attempt to emulate the accompanying thug lifestyle. Even if he is one day released, his grandchildren will hopefully wonder what the precise allure of his lifestyle of criminality ever was.

**Jose Solis, Jr. Murder Site (Lil Danger):
Quality Inn, 110 East Fourth Avenue, Fourth Floor,
Spokane**

The Brief Extinguished Flame of Recording Artist Little Willie John

Little Willie John was a renowned rhythm and blues artist who influenced musical contemporaries such as Aretha Franklin and James Brown. His legacy is predominately buried and forgotten deep within historical music archives.

In the late 1950s, his hits such as *All Around the World*, *Need Your Love So Bad* and *Fever* elevated his popularity. More prominent artists and bands including Peggy Lee, Fleetwood Mac and the Beatles would later record some of his songs.

John was a combustible talent fueled by excessive drinking that ultimately derailed his career. He was born in rural Arkansas, one of ten children and grew up in Detroit where his father was a factory worker. His siblings formed a touring gospel singing group. Renowned record producers Johnny Otis and Henry Glover noticed him. Glover signed him to a recording contract under King Records.

He burst out into the popular music scene in 1955 and was nicknamed *Little Willie* due to his short stature. His talent and performances were substantial, but his temper and alcohol abuse became self-destructive.

John was popular in the Pacific Northwest after many years of touring. He arrived in Seattle during October 1964 after skipping bail in Miami for assaulting a man with a broken bottle.

His pattern of binge drinking escalated and on the particularly insane Saturday evening of October 17, 1964, he sabotaged the final remnants of his career and liberty. The evening before, his performance at a local club was a disastrous drunken debacle.

He began the evening intoxicated at a Central district dance hall. He jumped on stage to perform a few impromptu songs. He was chauffeured to a nearby house party accompanied by two local women during the early morning hours. The festivities shifted location a few blocks away to another residence.

The trouble began when a brawl erupted and Willie was punched in the mouth by a towering and burly ex-con named Kenneth Roundtree. John retaliated by knifing him to death. The 26-year-old was arrested and charged with manslaughter. He posted bail and continued touring unconcerned about the ultimate consequences.

At his January 1965 trial, he was found guilty. He appealed the verdict for the next 18 months. He lost his appeals and finally entered the State Penitentiary in Walla Walla in July 1966, facing an 8-20 year sentence.

Wild, uninhibited and unbound birds such as John wither in confinement. Within less than two years, he reported to the infirmary with pneumonia. He was locked into a Maximum Security isolation room. He died on May 26, 1968 at the age of 30 from a reported heart attack. Speculation suggested that the actual cause may have been from a beating or simple neglect in response to his illness.

Posthumously, Little Willie John was inducted into the Rock and Roll Hall of Fame in 1996. His intended comeback album entitled *1966* wasn't released until 2008. He recorded the album while appealing his conviction. It was poorly received by an industry that had shunned and forgotten the vocalist decades before.

**Little Willie John Fatal House Party Killing:
918 23rd Avenue, Seattle**

Mia Zapata and the Randomly Silenced Voice of the Street

The vibrant Seattle music scene of the late 1980's and early 1990's launched several locally based bands and artists into international prominence. Classified as *Grunge Rock* due to the informality of the artists' appearances and demeanor, Seattle briefly distinguished itself as a creative center heralded by such acts as *Nirvana*, *Pearl Jam* and *Soundgarden*.

Entrenched amidst the predominantly male swagger of the movement, singer Mia Zapata fronted a band called *The Gits*. Despite the frayed and earthy impression conveyed by most grunge performers, Zapata was raised amidst affluence and the parochial school system of Louisville, Kentucky. The street edge she conveyed by her aggressive lyrics and confrontational performances were studied and possibly a rejection of her privileged background. The singer was respected, revered and an ideal feminist icon who elevated her band from the modest underground club scene to a higher level of industry visibility.

Tragically, the charismatic Zapata would neither lead the band beyond local obscurity nor enjoy the renown of some of her contemporaries.

During the early morning hours of July 7, 1993, Zapata was spotted leaving a Capitol Hill district tavern. Afterwards, she briefly visited a friend living a block away on the second floor of an apartment building where she lived in the basement. What followed that visit and her activities afterwards have remained unclear. Witnesses remember her wearing headsets and listening to music that would have made any stranger's approach inaudible.

At 3:00 a.m. screams were heard two blocks from the tavern. A half hour later, her body was discovered dumped on a corner in the adjacent Central District in a ritualistic crucifix position. Police concluded she had been beaten, strangled and raped. She died from internal injuries suffered from the beating.

The case remained unsolved for ten years, despite fundraising efforts and extensive private and police investigations. The randomness behind the act offered no tangible clues.

Modern forensics would answer a seemingly irresolvable puzzle. A DNA sample of her killer's saliva had been left on Zapata's body. The DNA profile was extracted and maintained in cold storage until STR technology was developed with matching capabilities.

In 2001, an original matching attempt failed to generate any positive comparisons. In 2002, Florida fisherman Jesus Mezquia entered the national databank CODIS after being arrested for burglary and domestic abuse. He had an extensive history of violence towards women along with burglary, assault and battery. Mezquia had originally arrived into the United States in 1980 via a Cuban boatlift when President Fidel Castro released hundreds of violent felons into the open waters of the Caribbean Sea.

Mezquia's profile matched the DNA sample. Questions remained as to why he was in Seattle during 1993 and if he had any connection with Mia Zapata.

He was arrested for her murder in 2003. His appearance in Seattle was traced via a recorded report of indecent exposure charges on file against him in the city within two weeks of the murder.

His criminal trial a year later revealed little. It was speculated that he had likely stalked Zapata following her exit from the apartment or tavern. It was surmised that he had grabbed and dragged her to his car before assaulting her in the back seat. Mezquia did not testify in his defense and simply maintained his innocence. The convicted predator was condemned to 37 years in prison initially before appealing his sentence. The term was reduced by a single year. He remains incarcerated at the Stafford Creek Corrections Center in Aberdeen, close to the sea, but far from humanity.

In the volatile music industry, success is transitory. The Seattle music scene has receded in novelty and relevancy. Grunge has faded from fashion. Time and trends evolve and the rebellion of youth is expressed by a fresh generation of angst. The urgency of Mia Zapata's lyrics and rage perhaps remain poignant to the lives she transitorily influenced.

Their ranks have become fewer and concerns different. Many have long since replaced social upheaval with parental responsibilities and the normal shifting of life's priorities. Angry young demands for radical change have been displaced by urges oriented towards upward social mobility.

The Gits group disbanded following the demise of their lead singer.

**Mia Zapata's Body Discovery:
100 Block of 24th Avenue South, Seattle**

The Abruptly Silenced Voice of Radio Activist Mike Webb

Mike Webb did not live long enough to enjoy the entire social implementation of his gay right activism. Webb was an outspoken San Francisco and Seattle radio personality who began as a reporter and later became a controversial liberal talk show host.

His highest priority issue involved gay rights. During his San Francisco stint, he elevated his recognition by his on-air reporting of the 1978 murders of Mayor George Moscone and City Supervisor Harvey Milk by ex-Supervisor Dan White. Working from a radio station located blocks away from the City Hall shooting, he broadcast reports perched upon the station's rooftop.

When a jury found White guilty of voluntary manslaughter rather than the anticipated first-degree murder charge, outraged citizens overwhelmed City Hall, destroying buildings, setting fires and overturning police cars. The spontaneous protest became known as the White Nights Riots. Newscasters from various television and radio networks joined Webb at his ideal vantage point to broadcast the unfolding events.

These broadcasts peaked his prominence in San Francisco. Afterwards he bounced around as an on-air personality for several stations. By the 1980s, Webb relocated to Seattle and hosted talk shows at multiple stations. He was the program director for two different stations between 1984-1994.

Webb's aggressive and abrasive demeanor and uncompromisable demands for immediate change were not universally well received. His strident gay advocacy preceded a societal shift by several years. Seattle was a receptive and progressive audience. Change did not evolve quickly enough in his estimation.

His elevated moral podium then suffered a major dent. In February 2007, he was found guilty of making a fraudulent insurance claim after an automobile accident. He was fined and sentenced to perform community service. After the verdict was announced, he was fired from radio station KIRO where he'd been a fixture since 1996.

He continued to produce an Internet webcasted talk show called the GayBC Radio Network tackling controversial advocacy issues and events.

Abruptly he ceased production of the talk show on April 13, 2007. He appeared to have vanished without announcement or explanation. His sister reported him missing. She sensed he was in danger, but had no idea of his whereabouts.

He remained missing for two and half months without contacting anyone. His property manager assumed that he had simply abandoned the property. The house had been ransacked but his belongings remained intact. Police had sent out a cadaver dog, but nothing turned up.

On June 28, 2007, an employee of the property firm searched his Queen Anne residence and made a gruesome discovery. Webb's decomposed body was located in a crawl space wrapped in a blue plastic tarp and positioned underneath numerous storage boxes.

His autopsy revealed evidence of *multiple sharp force traumas* resulting from being axed to death in his sleep. A lover, Scott White, 28, who'd reportedly known Webb since the prior November, became the prime suspect. During Webb's absence, White hosted numerous parties on the property and had the indiscretion to brag about the murder to other transient attendees.

The combative Webb's alternative lifestyle or perhaps his generosity proved his undoing. He was reportedly attempting to wean White off his advanced drug addiction.

Scott White was convicted of second-degree murder and sentenced to twenty years in prison. He is currently serving his term at the Monroe Correctional Complex.

Many of the issues Mike Webb had fiercely advocated on behalf of the gay community would begin to materialize within the subsequent decade. These milestones included expanded hate crime legislation, domestic partner rights and gay marriage. His vocal contribution was silenced but the movement ultimately advanced behind fresh voices and successors.

Mike Webb's Murder Site:
2505 3rd Avenue W, Seattle

The Weighty Complexity In Executing Killer Mitchell Rupe

There was little humorous about the life and exploits of Mitchell Rupe.

In 1994, he became the butt of national news jokes when a federal judge upheld his murder conviction but agreed with Rupe's contention that by weighing more than 400 pounds, he was too heavy to hang. The risk of decapitation was too great in the opinion of the ruling judge, who decided the act would constitute cruel and unusual punishment.

Rupe was a convicted murderer responsible for the shooting death of two bank tellers in Olympia on September 17, 1981. The robbery and killings of Candace Hemmig and Twila Capton were particularly idiotic because Rupe was a regular customer and both tellers knew him. The bank branch was located in a remote temporary trailer near the county courthouse. It has since been removed and only an overgrown vacant lot remains.

During the armed robbery, he felt obliged to shoot both women at close range to eliminate witnesses. His take was $4,000. He forgetfully left his checkbook behind and was arrested the same day.

He was initially convicted of first-degree murder and sentenced to death. Entering prison, he weighed approximately 300 pounds. This level was sizable but certainly supportable for a noose. Hanging at that time was the primary means of execution in the state.

During his initial thirteen years of captivity, his weight ballooned in excess of 425 pounds. His attorney blamed the gain on a myriad of physical problems prompting fluid swelling, common with liver disease. The excess weight ultimately kept him alive, enabling him to evade his scheduled execution date.

Once he was spared hanging, emergency surgery was performed. The procedure allowed him to shed 150 pounds of fluid within a few weeks. As a result of his case, Washington's legislature in 1996 changed their primary means of execution to lethal injection.

Throughout the remainder of his incarceration, he successfully appealed his death sentencing twice. In one of the trials, a jury voted 11-1 for imposing the death penalty but could not sway the lone dissent vote.

Rupe's health ultimately worsened from his liver disease prompting multiple health complications. His attorneys pronounced him on the verge of death on multiple occasions beginning in 1995. This rationale became their reasoning for canceling his execution. His health kept rebounding but his weight remained excessive. He married in 1997, but was unable to received conjugal visits due to changes in the prison visitation laws.

Finally on February 7, 2006, Rupe's liver failed permanently. For over a month he had remained in the Walla Walla State Penitentiary prison hospital nearly comatose until he expired. His autopsy confirmed the terminal liver disease, advanced cirrhosis and hepatitis C. His weight had lowered to 260 pounds by the time of his death.

Upon the news of his demise, the families of his two victims were ecstatic. They indicated Rupe had exhibited no remorse during the subsequent years following the killings. His own attorney disagreed. He typified him as a *gentleman*, *intelligent* and *regretful for his actions*.

Perhaps his main regret, as with so many condemned individuals, was that he lacked the intelligence to adequately plan a crime and then evade capture.

Former Site of Bank Trailor

Nathan *Trigger* Gilstrap: The Gangland Intrusion Into Our Neighborhood Fortresses

Twenty-nine-year-old Nathan *Trigger* Gilstrap was fatally shot around midnight on July 13, 2010 in front of a Central Spokane residence. He ran several feet after impact before collapsing on the adjacent neighbor's lawn where he died.

Gilstrap had lived an unremarkable life and was known primarily for his gang association and criminal convictions. He'd been involved in seven theft-related felonies dating back to 1995. He'd been out of custody nearly a month after being sentenced to 14 months for criminal impersonation.

Gilstrap was a witness to a fatal stabbing the previous summer of a local 24-year-old gang member. The victim's offense? He yelled something at his killers' passing car. Gilstrap helped police identify the suspects who he'd been drinking with earlier and was not charged in the death.

Amidst the insulated world of gangland violence; clothing, taunting and graffiti tagging may constitute capital offenses, punishable by death. Each act symbolizes a lack of respect to these clandestine and illegal groups that themselves remain defiant to organized society's standards and laws. The contradiction is obvious.

Three years after the slaying, police informants fingered two individuals who they claimed were responsible for Gilstrap's shooting. Their evidence was based on hearsay conversations and paranoid behavior exhibited by one suspect who reportedly Gilstrap owed money to. Police felt there was not enough substantial evidence to arrest either party. Predictable denials of guilt and even knowledge of the victim were attributed to the suspects. One of these individuals was later arrested in a March 2014 raid on federal charges involving the manufacture and sale of opiate drugs in a network spanning four states.

The murder weapon used on Gilstrap was recovered nearby in an alley. Forensics officials indicated that DNA evidence was present. Despite its presence, no subsequent arrests have been made.

An Internet message board focused on Northwestern Pacific gang activity posted that Gilstrap was a member of the Sureno gang. The origins of the group are traced back to the Mexican Mafia and state and federal correctional facilities. Their recruitment base has traditionally been southern California but participation now extends throughout the United States.

The expansion of youth and young adult gangs should not be surprising to habitual viewers of television and films, listeners of popular music and wearers of contemporary fashion apparel. The gang influence is unmistakable. Regionally, gangs are often loosely structured. Their affiliations may be more symbolic than accountable to a central organized hierarchy.

Their activities have extended beyond traditional illegal drug distribution, extortion and prostitution. White-collar crime has become a growth industry concentrating on credit card fraud, embezzlement and identity theft. The financial stakes and potential returns are significantly greater. The risk of capture is reduced since much of the activity is online. Convictions rarely result in the extended or lifetime sentencing of violent offenses and murder.

Law enforcement agencies significantly lag behind in tracking and eradicating these activities. Many of these organized crime enterprises have evolved into multi-million dollar syndicates.

Nathan *Trigger* Gilstrap was a lowly disposable foot soldier in this warfare between society and criminality. How he earned his nickname was never publicly clarified, but speculation seems obvious. His soon forgotten legacy became simply yet another young male fatality and unsolved murder.

Police departments nationwide, due to budget constraints, have been compelled to reduce personnel and operations. Specifically targeted for cuts are neighborhood bureaus and resource officers. Gang presence and proliferation in troubled sectors is reemerging. The identifying signs become noticeable when they linger. Spray-painted graffiti tags remain, drug and prostitution houses emerge along with intimidating assaults against defiant neighbors.

A more subtle and dangerous presence however is the infiltration of criminal operations into middle class suburbia and upscale residences. By resembling and emulating traditional American family units, their identities become difficult if not impossible to distinguish. Their loyalties, however, remain markedly different than their neighbors.

Recapturing a sense of security and law obeisance in Spokane and other American cities becomes a block-by-block process. Apathy and neglect become easy recruiting environments for ensnaring impressionable teenagers and young adults. Easy money is always a motivating influence. The cycle of neighborhood decline rapidly follows from the inside core.

It is simplistic to assume that by relocating one's residence into more affluent demographics or simply ignoring the obvious the problem will resolve itself. The expansion of youth gangs and their newfound activities is proof enough. The infiltration of a new class of crime and criminal has already encroached into previously solid, stable and law-abiding environments. Territorial boundaries have now become irrelevant and the participants are no longer distinctively identifiable.

**Nathan *Trigger* Gilstrap Murder Site:
2105 West Boone Avenue, Spokane**

Patrick Gibson: A Tainted Hat Nearly Undermines A Cold Case Conviction

The November 7, 1992 robbery and shooting death of Spokane Valley furniture storeowner Brian Cole, 48, followed another hold up hours before in nearby Coeur d'Alene, Idaho. The same perpetrator had robbed a children's store with marginal results before the botched furniture store attempt. Cole's killing was prompted by the gunman's threat to harm his wife during the robbery. She ultimately witnessed his murder.

The killing went unsolved for 19 years before DNA from a fake beard left at the crime scene was traced to convict Patrick Kevin Gibson. A hat worn by Gibson was also left behind.

During the search before his apprehension, a 1993 re-enactment of the crime was broadcast on the television show *America's Most Wanted*. The emission produced no credible leads, but nearly derailed the prosecutions later efforts to convict Gibson. A sheriff's deputy, since retired, lent the hat from the crime scene to the show's production team. Show producer John Walsh and the actor who portrayed the killer, handled the hat during filming, compromising its value as evidence.

Patrick Gibson had an extended criminal career. He was convicted for armed robbery, rape and kidnapping in 1978 in Nevada and robbery and rape in Oregon in 1979. During that period, a law enforcement official shot him in the face during a chase in Utah. The distinctive wound probably explained his use of the fake beard.

He would be arrested again in 1996 in California for a string of bank robberies and initiate in federal prison the sole accomplishment in his sordid life. During his 12-year sentence, he was obliged to enroll in the federal witness protection program after informing on a former cellmate of a previous crime. He provided authorities with details about the murder of a mother and her two children in Iowa earlier in the decade. His assistance enabled the conviction of Dustin Honken to a first-degree murder change and death sentence.

Upon his arrest in 2011 and during his trial the following year, he attempted to attribute the fake beard to one of his bank robbery associates. A jury was unconvinced by the testimony of man whose background lacked credibility. The tainted hat was attacked by his defense as compromised evidence. The jury felt that other circumstantial evidence and the fake beard DNA was sufficient and convicted him.

The serial bank robber was sentenced to 41 years in prison and is currently interned at the Monroe Correctional Complex following a stint at the Clallam Bay Correction Center.

The sole remarkable aspect to this case was the ineptitude of the police department's evidence handling. Their exuberant but irresponsible cooperation with a television production crew nearly enabled a guilty man to elude the responsibility for his crime.

**Patrick Kevin Gibson Furniture Store Robbery and Killing:
Former Coles Furniture Store Site, 13917 East Sprague, Spokane Valley**

Two Child Killers Separated By City Blocks and DNA Profiles

Puget and Point Defiance Parks are located within a few miles of each other in the northernmost tip of Tacoma. Both are popular recreation areas and accommodating to bicyclists, families and picnickers. The more expansive Point Defiance Park features a zoo and aquarium within its 29 acres.

Petite and blond Michella Welch, 12 accompanied her two younger sisters to the diminutive and familiar Puget Park at 10:00 a.m. on March 26, 1986. At 11 a.m., she went to their house to prepare them lunch. When she returned to the park, she searched for her sisters who had simultaneously walked to a nearby business to use their restroom. When the sisters arrived back to the park, they could not locate Michella.

She was last spotted at 1:30 p.m. speaking with an unidentified man. Her sisters contacted the police who initiated a search. At 11:30 p.m. that same evening, a tracking dog discovered her body in a makeshift fire pit near the park. Her throat had been slit and she had been sexually assaulted.

A classmate told detectives that she saw a man viewing the girls that morning from under the Proctor Bridge. He was described as Caucasian and skinny and approximately 24-26 years old. Another sighting described a Hispanic man with black hair, mid-height and between 25-35 years old. A known Tacoma child killer was briefly arrested as a suspect, but released due to a lack of evidence. The case went frigid.

Five months later, Jennifer Bastian, 13 was riding her bicycle throughout the Point Defiance Park. When she didn't arrive home that evening, her family called the police. Hundreds of people participated in her search. Three weeks later, her body was discovered concealed in underbrush. Her bike was hidden nearby. It was presumed that she had been sexually assaulted.

Both cases appeared related, but neither yielded any serious leads. The assumption made was that the killer had previously been convicted of another sex crime or murder. Police continued to search for a single individual. Both cases were eventually assigned to a special cold case division established in 2009 by the Tacoma Police Department.

Despite voluminous files for both cases, initial progress was slow and laborious. Over 2,300 males were referenced in the files. Police possessed a DNA profile for Michella Welch's killer. Nothing matched on the FBI's national criminal database.

Jennifer Bastian's case was even more problematic. Her body decomposition by the time of discovery left nothing traceable. In 2013 on a hunch, investigators decided to examine her swimsuit for DNA traces. If she had indeed been sexually assaulted, her swimsuit would have had to be lowered. The suit was found around her ankles when the body was originally recovered.

The lab sent the swimsuit out for testing and male DNA was discovered. The biggest shock was that it was different from Michella Welch killer's DNA sample. The assumption of a single killer turned out to be false. Separate perpetrators were responsible for each girl's death.

Throughout the next five years, the cold case unit employed advanced DNA techniques, forensic genealogy and collected DNA samples from 160 men. The process ultimately resulted in the May 2018 arrest of Robert Washburn for the killing of Jennifer Bastian. He pleaded guilty to first-degree murder charges in January 2019 and was sentenced to 27 years in prison. He is currently interned at the Washington State Penitentiary in Walla Walla.

Washburn, a Tacoma native, navigated for decades invisibly. He was 28 at the time of the abduction and murder and worked as a mechanic for Boeing. He lived two miles from the park and often jogged there. He had been arrested in 1985 in King County on suspicion of vehicle prowling and criminal trespass, but never charged. His father formerly owned a body shop in Tacoma. He had been married twice.

He filed for bankruptcy in 2000 while living in Burlington, Washington and relocated to Eureka, Illinois around 2005. He remained unemployed and the sole caretaker of his disabled daughter in her 20s. In one of several bizarre ironies, back in 1986 Washburn had phoned in a tip regarding the murder of Michella Welch. Was his intention to steer police towards another suspect to assume responsibility for both killings? Did he actually know the other killer?

At his trial, Washburn, now 60, for the initial time faced Jennifer's family and some of her childhood friends. Her sister characterized Washburn best: *I certainly didn't expect the person who committed this crime to seem so old and small and weak. It's definitely not what I pictured*

In May 2018, 66-year-old Gary Charles Hartman was arrested and charged with the murder of Michella Welch. The killer's DNA on record was uploaded to a genealogical website that created a prototype *family tree* based on a match to one of the killer's relatives. The connecting chain led them to Hartman and his younger brother. Hartman's current DNA sample was obtained from a brown paper napkin he had used while lunching with a co-worker.

In 1986, Hartman lived two miles from Puget Park in a two-story house overlooking Commencement Bay. Washington's Department of Social and Health Services hired him in October 1998 as a registered nurse. In recent years, he worked at the Western State Hospital in Lakewood as a community nurse specialist. He resided in Lakewood with his third wife on the shores of Lake Steilacoom. He had no prior criminal record and had spent his entire life in Pierce County.

From the outset, Hartman insisted upon his innocence through his attorney. At his June 2018 arraignment, he pleaded *not guilty* to first-degree murder charges. A specific trial date has not been announced.

The strangest aspect amongst many odd coincidental elements to this case was the residence in 1986 of both men. Gary Charles Hartman lived on the 4600 block of North Huson Street and Robert Washburn on the 3100 block of North Huson. Whether they were ever acquainted has not been determined. The oddest coincidence will occur if Hartman is found guilty and shares the identical fate as Washburn.

**Puget Park Abduction and Murder (Michella Welch):
3111 North Proctor Street, Tacoma**

Point Defiance Park Abduction and Murder (Jennifer Bastian):
5400 North Pearl Street, Tacoma

Edward Scott McMichael: The Silencing of A Whimsical Tune

Edward Scott McMichael was a Seattle based musician whose professional credentials included the Bellevue, Everett and Cascade Symphony orchestras.

His most popular renown, however, was outside of Seattle's performing and sports venues including the Kingdome, Key Area, McCaw Hall, Safeco Field and Qwest Field. McMichael was more commonly know as Tuba Man, an innovative and inoffensive fixture. He was capable of improvising humorous melodies as the mood, crowd and circumstance dictated. The pocket change or dollar bills he might earn for his impromptu performances paled in proportion to the smiles and good feelings he stimulated with his audiences.

Near midnight on October 25, 2008, a group of teenagers randomly beat and robbed McMichael at a bus stop near the Seattle Center. He was viciously punched and kicked while lying vulnerably on the ground. He was treated at a local hospital, but succumbed to his injuries a week later.

The tubist's death did pass unnoticed. A Seattle columnist wrote an inspiring front-page article eulogizing McMichael's life and death. A memorial service was organized nine days after his death that was attended by approximately 1,500 mourners. His goodwill and memory had softened numerous hearts and sensibilities. The ceremony heralded him in the only suitable manner possible, with song and respect.

Sentencing justice wasn't pronounced for the responsible perpetrators. Three of the teenagers were sentenced to detention for manslaughter. Two of them were for 72 weeks and the other, only 36 weeks. Their abbreviated sentences were a legal travesty and tied exclusively to their age. Two other suspects were never identified or located.

Although justice did not prevail with the sentencing, karma did with one of the killers. Ja'mari Alexander-Alan Jones would murder DeShawn Milliken after inciting a fight at a Bellevue nightclub on Christmas Eve, 2012. The calloused and by then hardened Jones was sentenced to 18 years in prison and is currently jailed at the Stafford Creek Corrections Center after a stint at the Clallam Bay Corrections Center.

The sad death of Tuba Man represented more than just a passing of whimsical entertainment. For Seattle residents and visitors, it became the loss of a sincere dose of humanity.

**Tuba Man's Beating Site:
Mercer and 5th, Avenue Bus Stop, Seattle**

William Batten: A Lifetime of Sexual Abuse Provoked Incarceration

William Batten has spent over forty years of his life incarcerated for the stabbing death of two female teenage hitchhikers on the Moclips coastline. He is currently imprisoned at the Stafford Creek Corrections Center after a stint at the Washington Corrections Center in Shelton.

The killings became a sad culmination to his twisted beginnings and history of sexual perversion.

On April 18, 1975, the semi-nude bloodied bodies of two Tacoma women Guelisa Burton, 18, and Tina Lynn Jacobsen, 19, were found on top of their sleeping bags. They lay inside a makeshift shelter amidst piled driftwood along the Moclips River near the ocean beach. Each victim's hands were bound with twine. Their autopsies indicated that both had been killed days earlier as a result of deep penetrating stab wounds that had severed their major arteries.

At the crime scene, Batten had mistakenly left an electricity bill receipt along with an accompanying envelop addressed to his wife. At the same time this evidence was being discovered, investigators were conducting a house-to-house search for clues near the crime scene. In the course of their inquiries, they interviewed Batten, who was employed at a nearby Aberdeen shingle mill.

Batten and his wife lived with his parents approximately one half mile away from the murder. During the course of an interview, his father indicated that his son had recently picked up a couple of female hitchhikers, unaware of the significance. When shown a photograph of the two dead women, Batten admitted that one might have resembled a hitchhiker he'd picked up.

William Batten's sexual history was well known to the Gray Harbor County Sheriff's Office. His dossier revealed that on February 15, 1967, he had been committed to the Western State Hospital as a sexual psychopath. He had been arrested on charges of indecent liberties and burglary. Several teen-age children had accused him of being a voyeur and others indicated that he had threatened them with a knife. In November of 1974, he had faced allegations of child abuse and molestation.

Within a week of the killing, he was arrested by authorities for the double murder and confessed. According to his recorded statement, he had picked up the women earlier in the day and transported them a bluff where they had assembled their makeshift campsite. He returned later in the evening and managed to subdue and tie down both. One of them screamed for assistance. He slashed her in retaliation. In the fury that followed, he killed both women to avoid having witnesses.

At his trial, Batten was convicted on two counts of first-degree murder and sentenced to life in prison. In 1977, Batten would file an unsuccessful appeal arguing that he was deprived of a fair process due to several pretrial and trial errors. His claims cited that evidence was improperly seized from his residence, his own hair was unlawfully examined and false testimony by an expert witness was prejudicial against him.

He remains a suspect in the 1969 disappearance of a woman he had formerly dated. He will die in prison having never experience a life free of the complications resulting from a life inundated by sexual deviancy.

**William Batten Killing Site:
Beach Bluffs Near Moclips**

Alex Baranyi and David Anderson: The Thrill of the Kill

Seventeen year-olds Alex Baranyi and David Anderson were bored and restless. In November of 1996, both had dropped out of the Off Campus School in Bellevue, a local alternative high school. Prior to that, they had attended Bellevue High School.

Baranyi had left home following his parent's separation and relocation to the East Coast. His best friend Anderson had left home and moved in with friends. Their lives were on hold, which enabled them to spend most evenings hanging out at a local bowling alley and various restaurants. With so much time to kill, they became immersed with a fantasy and gothic subculture.

They cultivated an antisocial appearance and behavior, which found its manifestation in the late evening January 5, 1997 strangulation, stabbing and clubbing of 20-year-old Kimberly Ann Wilson. They concealed her body afterwards amidst the shrubbery of the Woodridge Water Tower Park in Bellevue. The following morning two boys playing in the park discovered her.

On the same day, after murder investigators had canvassed the crime scene and determined the identity of the Kimberly Wilson, they drove three blocks to inform her parents.

Three cars were parked in the driveway and their Christmas lights were still on. The house appeared dark inside. No one answered their knocks. One of the detectives canvassed the house and found a sliding glass door unlocked.

He entered the house and announced his arrival. He was greeted by silence. He roamed inside and mounted the upstairs hallway. Entering the second level, he viewed blood splattered over the walls and ceilings. In the master bedroom, he found the body of Rose Wilson bludgeoned to death from blows to the skull and repeated stabbings. In the same room at the base of another bed, he found the body of William Wilson killed in the same manner.

Further down the hall in another bedroom laid the lifeless body of Julia Wilson. Unlike her parents, she had defensive stabbing and slashing wounds on her hands indicating that she had struggled with her attacker(s).

The city of Bellevue was considered serene, affluent and secure. In the 1990s, it was also close knit. The police acting on a tip brought in Alex Baranyi for questioning. He immediately confessed to the murders. He indicated that the rest of the family was killed because they were aware of Kimberly's friendship with David Anderson and their meeting the evening of her death.

Kimberly Wilson's selection as victim may have been impulsive and arbitrary. Investigators later theorized that Baranyi and Anderson simply murdered her for *the sheer experience of killing*. Money may have also been a motivator.

Kimberly Wilson had a crush on David Anderson, even with their age difference. Despite his lukewarm interest towards her, she lent him money periodically. Shortly before her killing, she had requested Anderson to repay back the monies. He claimed to be outraged by the request.

Baranyi and Anderson were tried separately.

Baranyi was tried first and confessed to killing Kimberly and Julia Wilson by strangulation. He stated that Anderson had killed Rose and William Wilson with an aluminum baseball bat. Psychologists attempted to explain Baranyi's actions based on his depression and a bipolar disorder condition. His jury held him fully accountable for his actions. After a three-week trial, he was found guilty on four counts of aggravated first-degree murder. He was sentenced to four consecutive life sentences without the possibility of parole. He is currently interned at the Clallam Bay Correctional Center.

Anderson's trial strategy was an attempt to distance his actions from Baranyi's. He rationalized the impulsive murder of Kimberly over his outrage that she'd demanded repayment of her money. He had considered the sum a gift. This tact was an attempt to downplay any premeditation and explain his actions as manslaughter. He denied having anything to do with the family massacre.

His tactic backfired when a friend testified that Anderson had invited him to join the pair the same evening to commit the family carnage.

His initial trial resulted in a hung jury due to one defiant juror voting against conviction. The case was retried. Anderson changed his attorneys. A second jury convicted him on all four counts of aggravated first-degree murder. He was sentenced to four consecutive life sentences without the possibility of parole. He is currently interned at the Monroe Correctional Complex.

Whatever pleasure either killer received by their actions, the infinity of lingering time has long ago ceased the novelty. Both are now surrounded by convicted murderers whose own histories of mayhem horrify and exceed their four impulsive killings.

They can never reverse their actions any more than one day return to a freedom they squandered.

Woodridge Water Tower Park, Kimberly Wilson's Murder Site:
1843 125th Avenue SE, Bellevue

**Wilson Family Murder Site:
1521 121st Avenue SE, Bellevue**

A Fatal Stabbing Of One of Society's Forgotten

Barbara Hickey, 57 was a familiar face to Bremerton's paramedics with her seizure disorder. The condition may have originally begun from an injury when she was younger. When she neglected to take her medicine, she would convulse and become disoriented until paramedics could stabilize her at a hospital. It became a ritual that was capable of repeating multiple times during a single one of their shifts.

Hickey seemed to be a woman without a past. She was visible to the first responder and medical community, but invisible to the majority of residents in a community preoccupied with their own existence. Hickey circulated amidst a small circle of local peers and played pool habitually in taverns. Her means were modest and what they shared amidst their companionship was a cruel loneliness, but acceptance of each other's frailties and disabilities.

Hickey indeed had a past that included a marriage, children and divorce decades before.

On the night of September 9, 1992, Hickey spent the evening at the *Drift Inn Tavern* in Bremerton. She spoke at length with a younger man in his 20s with collar length reddish-brown hair. He was a familiar face in town, but no one seemed to know his name. They left the tavern at closing time and took a cab together to her studio apartment.

Ten hours afterwards, she was found strangled and stabbed to death. A woman incapable of harming anyone was now a casualty from a poor partner selection.

The fingerprints left at her apartment led investigators nowhere. Her murder as her precedent existence became a low departmental priority over time. Absent of arrests and serious leads, the case went cold.

During the subsequent twenty-six years, forensic procedures evolved. Hickey's case was reopened and evidence found at the murder site was submitted to the Washington State Patrol Crime Laboratory for DNA analysis. No specific person matched this DNA profile, but a previously inconsequential clue coincided with another unsolved murder committed in Boise, Idaho in 1994. Lee Robert Miller's named surfaced within the files of both homicides, but not as a primary suspect. His name was written on a slip of paper that Barbara Hickey had carried in her purse.

Boise detectives tailed Miller and were able to retrieve a cigarette butt discarded by him. That DNA sample matched the profile for both unsolved murders. An arrest warrant was obtained in January 2019 and Miller was taken into custody. He pleaded guilty to the strangulation death of Hickey and the 1994 stabbing death of Cheryle Barrett in Boise. The combined second-degree murder pleas resulted in his receiving a minimum 42-year sentence before being considered for parole.

At the conclusion of sentencing, Miller apologized to both families for his actions. His defense attorney cited his difficult childhood with an abusive and alcoholic stepfather as a contributing factor towards his violence. He had apparently been involved in intimate relationships with both women before killing them. During the years following, he fathered two daughters but remained estranged. In 2016, he moved to Boise to be the primary caregiver to one of his daughters. At the time of his arrest, he was about to become a grandfather.

When society's forgotten are eliminated or commit atrocities, few pay attention beyond the immediate headlines of the act. There are no monuments inscribed to their memory or inspirational speeches lauding their impact to society. Instead there are only legions more destined to share their fate of anonymity.

**Barbara Hickey's Apartment:
404 Chester Avenue, Bremerton**

Maternal Homicide Based on a One-Sided Werewolf Attack

On Sunday afternoon March 5, 2017, Sheaen Smith, 31 made a 911 emergency call from his mother's duplex rambling on incoherently about werewolves and vampires. He indicated that he had just stabbed his mother multiple times because she was a vampire and he was an avenging werewolf.

When police arrived to Aurora Lee Buol-Smith's residence across the street from the Fairhaven fire station, they discovered her dead on the ground floor from twenty stab wounds. She also suffered defensive wounds on her hands from attempting to fend off the attack.

Days before the stabbing, Sheaen Smith had been treated and released at a local hospital for acute psychosis related to his methamphetamine use. His significant recent use had prompted *voices in his head*. At his initial arraignment, the voices reassured him that if he was able to pay his $1 million bail, he could return to his mother's duplex to stay until his trial. Not surprisingly, the judge disagreed. Their difference in opinion became moot when Smith was unable to post bond.

Smith was a mechanical contractor with no prior felonies prior to the murder. He had been convicted of a misdemeanor assault charge on his wife at the same duplex seven years previously. His wife eventually divorced him and he moved in with his mother.

At his August 2018 trial for second-degree murder charges, Smith pleaded *not guilty by reason of insanity*. His public defense attorney summed up his argument with: *There is no explanation for this case, other than he was insane. He had no motive to murder his mother. He was clearly in a state of psychosis.*

The judge agreed. Smith was declared *not guilty* of the murder charges and sentenced to an indefinite stay at Western State Hospital to receive mental health treatment. The judge's rationale for leniency was based on being *touched* by Smith's family and friends seeking help for him days before the murder.

Mustached with extended flowing locks and draping beard, Smith addressed the courtroom assemblage following the verdict. In a quiet voice he declared his gratitude to the attorneys who handled his case and family that still supported him by stating:

To all those who stuck with me and continue to love me, I give thanks for that. And also I want to give thanks to my good friend Jesus Christ because he did something amazing and I can only hope to achieve that.

**Aurora Lee Buol-Smith Residence:
1520 McKenzie Street, Fairhaven**

Marsha Weatter and Katherine Allen: Mount St. Helens Ash Buries Two Hitchhiking Shooting Victims

The May 18, 1980 cataclysmic eruption of Mount St. Helens became the most economically destructive volcano in the history of the United States. 47 Bridges, 250 homes, 15 miles of railways and 185 miles of highway were destroyed. The massive debris avalanche triggered by an accompanying earthquake carved out a horseshoe shaped crater in the center core. Volcanic ash and debris were concentrated 19 miles from the epicenter. Evidence of ash circulating the globe was reported within two weeks of the blast.

Fifty-seven casualties were directly attributed to the volcano. The majority were from a lumber camp located approximately eight miles from the explosion. The remaining deaths were entrenched residents and curious individuals failing to heed the numerous evacuation warnings.

Two hundred and fifty miles away in a field of sagebrush and wild grasses, the bodies of Marsha Ann Weatter, 18, and Katherine Jean Allen, 20, were positioned side by side. The two women lay sprawled and covered by three inches of falling residue. This shroud of ash effectively hid their bodies for eighteen months before a chance discovery by pheasant hunters.

The covering prevented animals from disturbing the remains. Their location was ten miles west of Moses Lake and only 150 yards north of Interstate Highway 90. Motorists passed daily en route between Seattle and Spokane. The 1981 autumn rains ultimately washed away enough of the debris to enable their discovery.

Weatter and Allen were both from Fairbanks, Alaska and completing the final segment of a nationwide hitchhiking tour. They were booked to fly home from Seattle a few days after their death. Both had been shot a single time and were fully clothed. Tests to determine if they were sexually assaulted were never publicly revealed.

Prior to their execution, they had attempted to solicit rides from transient truck drivers at a café in Ritzville. They chose poorly. The exact location of their killing could not be confirmed due to the passage of time. Investigators estimated they were killed approximately six weeks before the eruption.

The tragedy behind their death seemed amplified by the reality that after such an arduous journey and so close to return, they were never able to finally arrive home.

**Ann Weather and Katherine Jean Allen's Body Discovery:
10 Miles West of Moses Lake/Off I-90**

The Forgotten Unsolved Killing of Louis Bellessa

The sole unsolved murder case in Ellensburg history has defied resolution since 1972. The local cold case prompted a reinvestigation during January 2013, but evaded conclusive suspects. Time has obliterated the prospects for closure, as most of the potential witnesses are deceased and clues sparse.

During an evening in early October 1972, local downtown pharmacist Louis Bellessa, 51, failed to return home after work. His wife telephoned police who entered the shop and found his sprawled body. He had been shot twice in the head. An undisclosed amount of money and pharmaceuticals were missing from the store. Was the killing a simple robbery or revenge motivated?

It had been the only murder since 1951 in a town most noted for being the location of Central Washington University. The city is wedged in between Mount Rainier, the Okanogan-Wenatchee National Forest and larger population center of Yakima nearby to the south. Further east extends the sagebrush wilderness of the state's rural belt. The community radiates the epitome of serenity and security. Homicide and violent crime then, as now, remains an infrequent intruder.

Bellessa's former pharmacy site has since become absorbed into a contemporary art gallery along with an adjacent storefront. The building's notoriety remains unknown to the present tenant. Louis Bellessa is likely forgotten except to long-time residents.

The city modestly functions with an absence of comparative urban drama and crime due to its isolation. For residents, this stability remains their collective preference.

**Louis Bellessa Pharmacy Shop Murder:
410 North Pearl, Ellensburg**

The Invisible Streetwalkers Along Tacoma's Puyallup Avenue

Puyallup Avenue in Tacoma would appear an ideal haven for downtown sex workers recruiting clientele. AMTRAK train, Greyhound bus and regional and local streetcar service depots are situated mid-block. The Tacoma Dome, the largest regional indoor sports and performance venue is an easy walking block away.

An approximate six-block stretch of lower Puyallup Avenue leads to a permanently closed bridge and detour routing towards nearby Fife and the Port of Tacoma. This sector is composed of older industrial buildings and vacant lots. It radiates a grittiness and severity where sexual intercourse is for sale minus accompanying compassion.

Amidst this hostile environment between the years 1994 and 2010, at least five women and teens no longer practice their illicit solicitations.

No one disputes the danger associated with the sex trade. These five were composed of various races and not simply prostitutes, but mothers, sisters and daughters. Each has gone missing and their disappearance has left a cruel trail of grief and sorrow. Each of them worked the lower Puyallup strip.

One of most notorious prostitute murder suspects, Gary Ridgway, (Green River Killer) has been absolved of responsibility for their disappearances and probable deaths. Currently in Washington, there are approximately 1,800 missing persons statewide and 146 of these are women in Pierce County.

Ridgway joins a crowded field of killers that historically have preyed upon prostitutes. To society, theses women appear outcast and invisible. This presumption is accurate but not entirely true. They remain human with diverse motivations for entering such a potentially lethal occupation. Perhaps five separate killers are responsible. Perhaps a single serial killer.

The five women and their current ages (if still living) include Danielle Mouton (34), Jennifer Enyart (35), Debra Honey (58), Tami Kowalchuk (37) and Helen Tucker (52).

In October 2017 inside a wooded area of Pierce County, the discovery of a partial skull fragment stimulated renewed interest in the disappearances of the identified five. The momentum since the discovery has flagged and fresh leads towards each cold case has been relegated to lower priority status.

Without a body, investigative evidence becomes impossible. Without a sense of public urgency towards the fate of these women, their identities and fates become consigned to forgotten statistical footnotes. Spokane police required over a decade before finally arresting Donna (Douglas) Perry. However, they had discovered cadavers and DNA evidence to work from.

The widely visible sex trade along Tacoma's Puyallup Avenue continues unabated. No one will be astonished when the eventual missing women tally reaches double figures.

Lower Puyallup Avenue
Tacoma

Oleg Babichenko: An Explosion Prompting A Response of Silence

The intersection of East 28th Street and Grand Boulevard in the Rosemere neighborhood of Vancouver is tranquil and unassuming. Nothing remotely appears threatening, sinister or inviting intrigue throughout the modest neighborhood. Steady vehicle traffic passes the corner throughout the day and evening.

On October 31, 1997, Oleg A. Babichenko, a youthful appearing 28-year-old from the Republic of Georgia was seated inside his Toyota station wagon parked on the corner. At 7:30 a.m. an explosive device was accidentally detonated and a powerful bomb unleashed.

The explosion shook the entire neighborhood blowing debris onto roofs a block away. A neighbor ran over to the vehicle and saw the burly Babichenko lying over into the passenger seat. A fire had ignited on his head. The quick reacting neighbor extinguished the flames by beating it out resulting in severe burns to his hands. His actions came at great personal risk since igniting the car's engine could have prompted a secondary explosion.

No other spectator initially assisted until he had managed to pull the victim's head and torso from the car. Finally some of the onlookers helped free the man's feet.

By the time, the driver was entirely dislodged and Vancouver firefighters had arrived, the car was an inferno. Flames shot through the top skyward. The fire was extinguished and the vehicle left as a mangled and contorted wreck. Babichenko was killed from his shrapnel wounds and lay in the middle of Grand Boulevard until the body was removed by ambulance.

Few details regarding the cause, motive or even the victim were subsequently published. Babichenko was described only as an unassuming and polite individual. He operated a shop space in a cramped corrugated steel building specializing in auto repair. Two years before, he had briefly run an auto-wrecking yard in nearby Washougal. His clientele was exclusively Russian and he did not accept outside business. His operations were discreet and no one interviewed by the local press could offer any incisive insight. Reports of arguments, fights or disputes were nonexistent.

Babichenko had a few minor skirmishes with the local legal system primarily for failing to appear in court on traffic offenses. A domestic violence petition had once been filed against him, but was later dismissed.

His life resembled the blank profile of an invisible man. Then he was abruptly gone or perhaps conveniently removed.

The sole suspicious published fact police investigators released was that his ignition key for the Toyota was in his pants pocket. The results of a reported official investigation and explanation were never made public.

An online rumor later circulated that he was involved in a stolen car and chop shop ring and murdered by the Russian mob. There was speculation that he was tinkering with the bomb when it exploded. Yet the question persists. What would he be doing with a bomb in a quiet residential neighborhood near his own house?

Legitimate questions might have been raised from the suspicious circumstances behind his death. They seem to have been ignored. Instead only silence remains decades later and an absence of concrete answers.

Suicide was at no point considered a motivation. The case remains open but seemingly as frigid as the current state of diplomatic relations between America and Russia.

**Oleg Babichenko's Bomb Detonation:
Grand Blvd and East 28th Street, Vancouver**

Roseanne Pleasant and Valiree Jackson: The Dual Generation Probable Killing of A Mother and Daughter

Roseann Marie Pleasant was 35 years old when she was last seen in front of a Spokane convenience store on October 1, 1992. Given her professional status as prostitute, her disappearance was not remarkable. It did not evolve into a priority case at the time she went missing. Her body was never recovered.

Pleasant left behind a two-year-old daughter Valiree and a common law husband, William Bradley Jackson, a truck driver.

Barely seven years later on October 18, 1999, Jackson reported that Valiree vanished that morning from the front yard of her grandmother's home before attending elementary school classes.

Jackson became an immediate suspect when investigators discovered Valiree's blood on her bedsheets and her father's shoes. Worse, samples of his pubic hair were found in her bed. The Spokane police inserted a GPS transmitter into Jackson's truck without his knowledge so they could track his movements.

He soon led them to two fresh Spokane Valley gravesites. One was empty but still contained garbage bags, which had temporarily wrapped an object. The other one was filled with Valiree's nine-year-old body.

Once the body was discovered, the incredulous Jackson admitted to investigators that he had simply hidden his daughter but was not responsible for her death. He claimed she had died from an accidental overdose of the prescription drug Paxil, He affirmed to have panicked when he found her dead.

His story didn't make sense to investigators. The evidence instead suggested that Jackson smothered her in bed. They based his true motive on the theory that he was either sexually abusing her or she did not get along with his girlfriend.

The original second-degree murder charge was upgraded to first-degree murder during his trial. He was convicted and sentenced to a 56-year sentence based on the shocking nature of the crime. He is currently interned at the Clallam Bay Corrections Center.

On appeal, his attorneys claimed that the planting of the GPS device violated his constitutional rights. The appeal was overruled because the police had probable cause and had obtained proper judicial permission before installing the device.

Jackson has vehemently protested his innocence pleading he had no reason to kill his daughter who was *his whole existence*. Roseanne Marie Pleasant's family is convinced that not only did he kill Valiree, but her mother as well. Without a body, proof becomes problematic.

Without the GPS technology, it is probable he may have gotten away with murder twice in a lifetime.

**Roseanne Pleasant Disappearance:
Between Ash and Nora Streets, Spokane**

Susette Werner's Unimaginable Early Morning Dragging Death

Susette Werner, 42, left her habitual west central Spokane tavern with two men at approximately 1:30 a.m. on February 8, 2009. Patrons at the bar did not recognize either man, but both seemed familiar and comfortable with her.

Afterwards she reportedly visited a friend who worked at a nearby convenience store. What happened in the interim between her departure and approximately 3:45 a.m. when she was killed has never been determined. The two men she left the bar with were never identified nor any guilt established. Police believe Werner was hit by an automobile at a slow speed or was lying on the ground during the early morning hours.

Werner was struck at the intersection of Cedar Street and Carlisle Avenue. She was dragged south on Cedar, west on Northwest Boulevard and south on Ash Street to just before Maxwell Avenue, approximately 15 blocks. The driver stopped and backed up at the intersection of Ash and Maxwell, dislodging the body. She was found sprawled in the middle of the road. The driver vanished.

It has never been determined if the driver knew he was dragging a body for the entire mile-long distance. Her body was discovered at approximately 4 a.m. A witness who lived in the neighborhood described a suspicious dark sport utility van near the scene and furnished a description of the driver. He was approximately 6 feet tall and 300 pounds. He exited his vehicle briefly, scanned around that sector of Ash Street with a flashlight. Ten minutes later he made a telephone call and a station wagon arrived. The driver exited and the two men faced each other briefly before separating in their vehicles in different directions.

What transpired between the men was never determined. The witness was uncertain if they had even spoken with each other. Three days after the death, police released a distant color photograph of a black SUV published locally. The image generated no substantive leads.

Around the body, police discovered no evidence or discarded car parts, unusual for such a collision. Investigators were unable to determine if the dragging death was a homicide or an unfortunate accident.

Shortly after the tragedy, mourners created a makeshift memorial for Werner. They adorned a dirty snow pile at the intersection where she was hit with flowers, balloons and a wooden cross. The snow melted and another temporary remembrance was assembled on a metal fence at the corner of her discovery site. Vandals destroyed portions of the commemorative that Easter.

Despite an offered reward, no one stepped forward to claim responsibility or provide concrete leads. Both of Werner's parents were alive to grieve for their daughter's death. The mystery will never likely be resolved.

Was the tragedy purposely committed, a random accident or perhaps a product of intoxication by the culprit or victim? It is probable that the driver was simply too petrified to admit to an act that would cast immediate suspicions on his condition or inattention at the moment of impact. Only his conscience can address that question.

**Susette Werner's Vehicle Homicide:
Struck by vehicle at Cedar Street and Carlisle Avenue
and dragged until Ash Street and Maxwell Avenue,
Spokane**

Timothy Alioth and Donna Plew: A Double Homicide Mystery Within A Residential Oasis

The random inequity of homicide was never more evident than on the evening of February 6, 2009 in Vancouver. At approximately 7:15 a.m., driver Timothy Alioth, 58, and his passenger, sister Donna Plew, 62, were fatally shot in her driveway as both were exiting Alioth's pickup truck.

Alioth had been living at his sister's residence following a recent move from Oregon. Plew's husband had died on an airplane returning from Hawaii the previous September.

The killings appeared to be calculated and committed by someone both of them knew. The neighborhood had no prior history of violence. Neighbors spotted their lifeless bodies sprawled adjacent to their side doors after hearing three gunshots. There were no sightings of anyone fleeing the driveway or driving off hurriedly. The killer was likely awaiting their arrival.

Alioth had served from 1967 until 1973 as a corporal combat Marine along the DMZ in Vietnam. Both Alioth and Plew left behind children and grandchildren.

A police investigation remains currently void of a published motive and suspect. Two families are left with only unanswerable whys. The wait remains unbearable.

**Timothy Alioth and Donna Plew Murder Site:
7016 Indiana, Vancouver**

Chalisa Lewis: The Vanishing of a Young Poetic Soul

Chalisa Lewis had a beautiful poetic soul that ironically foresaw a personal calamity even she was unaware of.

On the morning of Thursday, February 2, 1995 she wrote in her diary: *Dear God, I know you have a reason for everything and it all works out in the long run but I just don't get it.*

Her words proved prophetic as she stepped off the school bus on her way home. She would never arrived to her destination and vanished without leaving behind any clues. Three weeks later, her body would wash ashore at Seattle's Discovery Park. Her death was ruled by the examining coroner as *saltwater drowning*.

The strange inexplicable case baffled investigators since there were no reports of violence preceding her abduction nor anyone at the time that witnessed her disappearance. Police speculated that she might have voluntarily accompanied her captor.

At her memorial service, her youth pastor described her as a young lady with *grave spiritual questions.* Her once bubbly personality had darkened over the past months, yet no one could pinpoint why. Her friends spoke glowingly of her as *gregarious* and *fun-loving* with an endearing habit of telephoning them the day before her birthday to remind them of the occasion.

The years have stretched out to over a quarter of a century and a motive for her murder remains as elusive as a prime suspect. Offered rewards did not stir fresh activity or arrests. One of the individuals who posted a reward indicated that he saw her getting into a car on the day of her disappearance.

Chalisa's great passion at fourteen was to compose sensitive and questioning poetry. What remained unanswerable to her would never become resolved. Five years after her death, her family had dispersed to Spokane and Montana. She would never celebrate her fifteenth birthday.

**Chalisa Lewis' Last Sighted Location:
900 Pacific Avenue, Bremerton**

Fred Cohen: The Perfectly Executed Murder of A Preeminent Local Attorney

Fred Cohen had known enemies. One finally killed him.

He was locally raised in Bremerton before attending the University of Washington where he graduated in 1936. After earning his law degree. He worked five years as a Kitsap County prosecutor. The first year he was appointed and then subsequently afterwards elected. In 1946, he opened his private practice specializing in civil cases. He integrated himself locally as a Shriner, Elks club member, leader of the Anti-Defamation League, Jewish Community Center and member of the Port Orchard Yacht Club.

Cohen was typified by his peers as *aggressive, very capable* and *a hard driver*. His verbal sparring earned him respect, but equally adversaries who chafed under his aggressive and often harsh manner.

On January 19, 1970, Cohen arrived at his home at approximately 6 p.m. in the pitch darkness. His car entered his property via an extended horseshoe driveway. He parked and strolled to his rear terrace via a connecting sidewalk. He stood at his rear door scanning the Port Washington Narrows. His wife was inside the house, but unaware of his arrival.

Cohen heard a distracting noise twenty-five feet away and reportedly turned to face a concealed gunman. The shooter fired a single shotgun blast into Cohen. The sound startled his wife who noted that she heard an accompanying laugh in the distance. She could see only pitch black from their dining room window. Scanning below, she viewed her husband lying mortally wounded.

The killer left no footprints on the beach and was presumed to have escaped via a pathway behind the house. Neither murder weapon nor expended cartridge were found.

Investigators immediately focused on Cohen's potential enemies. He had received death threats in the past due to his legal practice, but no one could be conclusively isolated as a prime suspect. Over the years, the leads dwindled and one of Bremerton's finest advocates became a forgotten casualty of a planned assignation.

**Fred Cohen Residence:
1412 Seventeenth Street, Bremerton**

A Surprising Suspect Emerges Amidst the Embers of A Cold Case Murder

James *Jimmy* Smith, 31 was a reliable custodian at Port Orchard's Hi-Joy Bowl for five years before his lifeless body was discovered on the morning of August 15, 1961. Smith was found lying on his back expired from two deep and sharp cuts to his head. Blood had flowed from wounds on both sides. The blows were delivered while he was prone and the killer wiped his hands and the bloody blade on Smith's sweatshirt.

Port Orchard's Police Chief Gale Dow and Chief of Detectives Glenn Pendarvis headed the investigation and theorized that Smith who often began his shift at 4 a.m. was killed when he surprised a burglar or burglars inside the building. A crescent wrench was discovered that was speculatively used to break the rear entry window. A footprint was found outside of the alley which investigators made a cast of. The safe remained shut, nothing was reportedly missing and the murder weapon not found. A nearby real estate and accounting office had been entered, but neither had anything taken of value.

Dow assembled an investigative force from various military and law enforcement agencies. Their search for clues, particularly an ax, hatchet or meat cleaver proved fruitless. Ultimately no suspects emerged based on the burglary theory. Dow remained tight lipped publicly about nearly all of the investigative leads and details. His suspicion leaned towards the perpetrator having chosen the site while passing through town.

In a follow-up article fifteen years later in the *Kitsap Sun*, Dow was still Police Chief, but would leave the office later that year. Bill Clifton was the new Chief of Detectives.

Both men still floated the theory that a burglar killed Smith, but Clifton theorized on a different tact.

He concluded that the murderer was a local resident and still living in the area. He speculated that Smith knew his killer and was slain to prevent identification. He elaborated on the extensive efforts that the department had undergone to uncover the murder weapon including draining a pond behind the bowling alley. He further added that investigators had found a cheap wristwatch on the scene with a broken band suggesting a struggle preceded Smith's death. The watch proved untraceable.

He concluded by adding *I've got two very excellent suspects. They're just jim dandies*, but he declined to elaborate or provide names.

On the 41st anniversary of Smith's murder, the *Seattle Times* did a follow-up article on the case. The article was stimulated by a public talk Bremerton city councilman Ed Rollman delivered at the Port Orchard Library in 2002 introducing a fresh suspect. Rollman was noteworthy for driving an old police cruiser and independently investigating crimes within Bremerton on his own time.

Many local circumstances had changed since the 1976 *Sun* article. The Hi-Joy Bowl had suffered a devastating fire requiring a complete overall and refurbishment. Police Chief Gale Dow had died at the age of 71 in 1997 after being sentenced to 20 years in prison in 1985 for statutory rape and indecent liberties. His name however remained affiliated with the Smith murder, but this time as a primary suspect.

Further details regarding the case emerged regarding Port

Orchard's only unsolved murder at the time. The most telling pointed to a *deliberate* homicide. Gale Dow and Jimmy Smith were frequently seen together at the bowling alley restaurant. The burglary motive proved dubious as $270 was discovered in the cash register and Smith's wallet remained tucked in his back pocket. The discovered footprint turned out to be Dow's and all of the case's acquired physical evidence had been stored in Dow's personal filing cabinet. When he left the force, so did all of the evidence.

The most damning rumors originated from Dow's second wife who suspected his guilt. She related to whoever would listen that he'd been out the entire night of the killing and returned home disheveled with blood on his uniform. She died the year before the *Times* article appeared.

A motive for Smith's killing still remains prone to speculation. Did he know too much about the police chief who oversaw Port Orchard with a fierce grip? Evidence has disappeared and inquiries have become limited to rumor and innuendo. Whoever was responsible for the custodian's death will never experience a day of judicial justice presuming he is deceased.

Dow's accuser Ed Rollman would complete his city council term the year following the *Seattle Times* article. He died abruptly two years later in his home at the age of 49. Gale Dow and Jimmy Smith have become faint and nearly forgotten memories within a contemporary Port Orchard neither would now recognize.

**Hi-Joy Bowling Alley
1011 Bethel Avenue, Port Orchard**

A Very Public Suicide on the Notorious Aurora Bridge

The George Washington Memorial Bridge in Seattle is locally called the Aurora Bridge and majestically spans State Route 99 over the west end of Lake Union. The viaduct connects the Queen Anne and Fremont districts and is nearly 3,000 feet long. Erected in 1932, the bridge has, due to its elevation earned the notorious distinction as a suicide launching point.

On November 27, 1998, Seattle Metro bus driver Mark McLaughlin and 34 passengers were heading south in an express lane to downtown. The extended accordion bus was cruising at a comfortable 50 miles per hour in the middle of the afternoon.

One of the passengers, 43-year-old Silas Cool approached McLaughlin and pulled out a .380 handgun. He shot the driver in the abdomen and then lifted the gun to his own head and fired.

Mark McLaughlin heroically steered the bus across two lanes of incoming traffic, hit a van and then plunged off the east side of the bridge. Had the bus fallen a mere 100 yards further, all of the passengers would have perished. Instead, the vehicle plunged onto the roof of an adjacent building ironically named the Troll Eye Apartments on 36th Street in the Fremont district.

The famed Fremont Troll, a mixed media colossal statue is located 100 feet kitty corner from the apartment complex and situated under the north end of the Aurora Bridge. The public sculpture, composed of steel rebar, wire and concrete, clutches a Volkswagen Beetle. His sole viewable eye is a hubcap as his hair covers the other. Thousands visit the Troll annually.

McLaughlin and Cool were dead upon impact. One passenger, Herman Liebelt later succumbed from injuries sustained in the crash. All of the remaining passengers were injured, some seriously.

New Jersey raised Silas Cool was a petty thief, vagrant and had exhibited a handgun to a passenger once before on another bus. Why he chose the day after Thanksgiving for his rampage remains a mystery.

McLaughlin was honored and decorated by the Metro bus service and his fellow drivers. He converted a certain catastrophe into a smaller scale tragedy. His fate and heroics accentuate the risk urban bus drivers face on a daily basis.

As a side note, the good fortune extended by the Fremont Troll to bridge passengers was severely re-tested in the fall of 2015 when five people were killed and fifty injured when an amphibious tour vehicle crashed into a charter bus. Two smaller vehicles were also involved in the crash, which was initiated by mechanical error and not criminal intent.

**Aurora Bridge Murder-Suicide Site:
East Side of Bridge/Apartment Building on 36th Street, Seattle**

Collective Grieving, Renewal and Hope Following An Unexplainable Rampage at the Café Racer

Patrons of Seattle's Café Racer Espresso are an eclectic mix of artists, musicians, political activists and fringe members of society. Creativity and eccentricity are embraced. The interior décor matches the libertine spirit of the intimate University of Washington district café.

No client was more erratic and opinionated than Ian Stawicki. His consistent rants, rudeness and aggressive antics had caused him to be banned from the premises.

Shortly before 11:00 a.m. on May 30, 2012, Stawicki walked into the café. Staff members recognized him and reminded him that his presence wasn't welcomed. He lingered, hesitated and then strolled towards the front door. He pulled out one of two .45-caliber handguns and shot a patron in the back of the head. His victim's body blocked the exit door.

One customer threw a bar stool at Stawicki and used another in an attempt to disarm him. Three patrons escaped in the melee. The stool proved only a temporary distraction to an armed man set on a killing rampage. He murdered three remaining patrons and wounded the café's chef, Leonard Meuse. Dead were regulars Donald Largen, Joe Albanese, Drew Keriakedes and Kimberly Layfield.

Exiting the café, Stawicki grabbed one of the victim's hats and headed towards the First Hill district of downtown. The owner of a SUV in the parking lot adjacent to the Town Hall Entertainment Complex made unfortunate eye contact with the deranged killer. Moments later, Gloria Leonidas was shot dead and her vehicle carjacked.

The manhunt for Stawicki continued relentlessly throughout the city. Finally sighted on a sidewalk in West Seattle around 4 p.m., police edged towards him and ordered him to drop his weapon, Stawicki lifted the gun to his head and emptied a chamber. He collapsed and died two hours later.

Stawicki had a minor history of violence and legal entanglements. No one close to him anticipated the extremity of the outburst. Firearms were part of his world and he had six handguns registered in his name. His most recent employment had been on a fish processing boat in Alaska. What ultimately triggered his final rage was never determined.

Despite the stigma attached to the shooting, the Café Racer remains open and welcoming to its outsider clientele. There was serious consideration towards simply closing the establishment by the owner. The enormity of the horror affected patrons, staff and anyone remotely connected to the café. A makeshift memorial was erected consisting of mementos, poetry, artwork and unusual objects. The accumulation filled the windowsills, sidewalk and stacked along the telephone poles. Informal large gatherings and impromptu concerts were held.

Over the subsequent eight years, the café opened and closed at least twice as the property was unable to secure a buyer, In August 2020, the property was definitively closed.

**Café Racer Massacre Site:
5828 Roosevelt Way NE, Seattle**

**Town Hall Entertainment Complex and Parking Lot
1119 8th Avenue, Seattle**

No One is Welcome in This Jungle

Seattle's *Jungle* is officially called the East Duwamish Greenbelt. The 160 acres extend underneath an elevated section of Interstate 5 from the periphery of South Dearborn Street until Lucile Street. The landmark boundaries begin from underneath the Interstate 90 and 5 bridge intersection until the western slope of Beacon Hill in southern Seattle.

The terrain of this urban *no man's land* is composed of heavily graffitied concrete freeway support pillars, shrubbery, berry brambles and vines. The greenery can in no manner be mistaken for a garden oasis. The weathered tents, trash, stray hypodermic needles and threatening ambiance make venturing into the interior dangerous sport.

Homeless encampments, rampant drug and alcohol use, mental illness and general lawlessness populate the *Jungle*. Periodically, the city initiates clean-up operations, employing bulldozers and demolition crews. The extent of the problem remains overwhelming and the eyesore blight resurfaces.

Amidst this chaos, the Taafulisia family resided for periods of 2015-16 in the shadows of Safeco Field (since renamed T-Mobile Park). The family unit was composed of James (17), Jerome (16) and a younger unnamed brother (13) residing with their mother, Lisa Valasi. She had been arrested in the past for selling crack cocaine, identity theft and shoplifting from a Goodwill store. Their father, a long time gang member and drug dealer is incarcerated.

The mother had previously lost custody of her three sons. Each had been relocated to foster homes. They preferred the symbolic unit of family, no matter how ghastly and escaped frequently from each of their assigned caregivers. There was absolutely nothing *heartwarming* about this reunion. The two older boys during their residence were being investigated in connection with previous robberies and a fatal shooting. Collectively the trio reportedly decided to reward their mother on her thirty-seventh birthday.

A *Jungle* drug dealer named Phat *Phats* Nguyen reportedly owed Lisa Valasi $500. The brothers decided to form their own collection agency. The trio dressed in leather with concealing masks and approached Nguyen's tent in the encampment on the evening of January 26, 2016. They were armed with a .45 caliber handgun.

Apparently suspecting nothing threatening, Nguyen requested the trio to approach the front of his tent. A small group surrounded a campfire nearby to ease the sting of the relentless January chill.

The shooting began rapidly and without provocation towards Nguyen. They fired in the direction of the campfire. Nguyen and two others were wounded during the fuselage. Jeannine Zapata (45) and James Quoc Tran (33) died from multiple gunshot wounds. The Taafulisia's reportedly escaped with approximately $200-$300 in cash and $100 worth of black tar heroin. Later they would joke together about the encounter.

A sixth potential victim sitting around the campfire was spared. The boys angrily confronted him and demanded his reaction to the shooting. He calmly responded: *I'm just an old man sitting by the fire and trying to get warm.* Their hesitancy to eliminate an eyewitness may have proven their undoing.

Within six days police arrested them. The youngest brother would idiotically sell the murder weapon to an undercover police informant erroneously thinking he might spare his brothers potential trouble with its disposal.

James and Jerome Taafulisia were convicted in December 2019 on two counts of first-degree murder. They were sentenced to 40 years in prison. Both are presently interned at the Ckallam Bay Corrections Center. The youngest brother was convicted of murder and assault in juvenile court. He will remain in custody until he turns 20.

Phat *Phats* Nguyen vanished following the shooting. Two of the wounded shooting victims have returned to their previous living niches. During the haunting pitch nights, many residents have begun to sleep in shifts for protective purposes. Guns and arbitrary violence stalk the shadows of any perceived calm. Some sleep with rifles or pistols within close access. The two murders were not particularly surprising, but even the most callous individual should be shocked by the ages of the perpetrators.

No one has effectively implemented a solution to the prolific global homeless crisis. Many of the marginalized and ostracized simply wished to be left alone. They are escaping from their past and a future that will terminate their lives prematurely. Compassionate and tolerant individuals cannot ignore the inhumanity, but even they have yet to make much impact on an obstinate resistance and intensified rebellion making constructive rehabilitation impossible.

Whether the *Jungle*, Georgetown district, South Seattle or the rear porch of the downtown Seattle Public Library during summer months, the homeless calamity is blatant and bare for our daily viewing.

**Seattle's Jungle:
East Duwamish Greenbelt, adjacent to Interstate 5
between South Dearborn and Lucile Streets**

Michael Feeney: His Fateful and Tragic Obsession

Obsession and jealousy fully erupted into its worst possible manifestation on the late evening of April 10, 2011 in Longview.

Michael Feeney, 44, had been married to Dana Enyeart, 39, for five years, divorcing in 2006. They had no children together. Both had daughters separate from their union. Their divorce appeared superficially amicable. The two had been spending time together, despite being five years removed from the marriage.

Still, he couldn't let go.

He suspected his wife had resumed dating and was seeing a former lover, Bruce Kamp, 36.

Kamp had become the caretaker for his ailing grandfather Willie Kamp. He rented out his own house and moved into the basement. The arrangement suited both men.

On the evening of April 10th, Feeney trailed Enyeart to Willie Kamp's residence, where she intended to spend the night with Bruce. Michael Feeney kept watch on the house. He paced between his pickup truck and the residence, working himself into a frenzy. When the couple retired into the basement together, he made a fateful decision. He retrieved a gun from his vehicle.

Feeney entered the house and crept towards the basement bedroom. He held the terrified couple at gunpoint and ranted for ten minutes. When derogatory names were no longer sufficient, he emptied seven cartridges into each of them. Willie Kamp discovered the bodies.

The killer drove to a friend's house and drank a beer, his final taste of freedom. He turned himself into the Longview Police.

At his trial he cried profusely and pitifully. He bathed in remorse and mumbled apologies to the hard-hearted assemblage. There could be no forgiveness, only intense hatred towards a cowardly and brutal act. Two families were forever ripped apart. One of his teenage daughters lent perspective when she spoke through tears *that one act does not define a person.*

It is ironic that although in principle she may be correct, Feeney's life will be defined by a singular impulsive act. He pleaded guilty to two counts of premeditated murder and one count of first-degree burglary. He was sentenced to a maximum life term of 70 years and is currently incarcerated at the Monroe Correctional Complex after a stint at the Washington State Penitentiary in Walla Walla.

Contentious divorce is considered one of the most traumatic experiences an individual may experience and endure. The process of severing two bonded lives is rarely seamless and without rancor. Michael Feeney could not imagine his ex-wife Dana happy in the companionship of another man. In the end, his bitterness and his inability to possess her cost him and two related families everything.

**Dana Enyeart and Bruce Kamp's Murder Site:
3038 Ammons, Longview**

Ali Muhammad Brown: Using Religious Fanaticism As A Pretext For Unspeakable Acts

Dwone Anderson-Young, 23, according to his mother, came out gay to her at the age of 14. He struggled through high school. After graduation, he enrolled in a program that enabled him to work during the day and take night courses at the University of Washington. He graduated with a degree in communications and began working in the IT department of a regional Medical Center. He had made ambitious plans for his life. He was fortunate to have a supportive mother who he lived with in Seattle's Leschi district.

On June 1, 2014, he went out with a friend, Ahmed Said, to a nightclub in the gay and lesbian friendly Capitol Hill district. Customarily, he returned home via cabs. That evening, Said was driving.

Said's parents were reportedly unaware of his sexual preference. The family bond however was very tight and strong.

Over the course of the evening, the pair encountered Ali Muhammad Brown reportedly through a cell phone app service designed to match gay partners and potential sexual liaisons.

Said consented to give Brown a ride home. Brown sat in the rear passenger section. Their first stop was a half block away from Anderson-Young mother's house. From the backseat, Brown pulled out a gun and opened fire without warning. He executed the pair with fatal shots to the head and back. The killings did not appear to be motivated by robbery, drugs or any other obvious reasons.

Brown fled the crime scene and the Seattle area. He would continue his rampage later in New Jersey where on June 25th, he murdered a college student-athlete Brendan Tevlin. In July, he was apprehended in a makeshift tent. He was found with the handgun used in all of his slayings.

After Brown's New Jersey arrest, King County sheriff's deputies linked him to a third Seattle homicide in the Skyway district. On April 27, 2014, he was accused of gunning down Leroy Henderson around midnight walking home from a nearby store. The shooting appeared random and without cause.

Brown confessed to all of the killings while being interviewed by police at a New Jersey detention center. His stated motivation was based on his interpretation of a Muslin faith that condemned American foreign policy and aggression in the Middle East. His rationale called for an even exchange of American and Arab deaths. He further stipulated his responsible homicides were targeted towards individuals committing evil acts. His doctrinal interpretation may ultimately qualify him for hate crime status in Washington and the death penalty upon his extradition. New Jersey has abolished the death penalty.

Gay and lesbian rights proponents have made significant strides in educating and securing acknowledgement for their traditionally alternative lifestyles globally. Their demands long ago surpassed simple acceptance. Today, discrimination is considered a violation of basic Civil Rights.

Approval has not been universal, particularly within more zealous religious ideologies and individuals advocating that homosexuality is an affront to their definition of *normal* behavior. This division in conscience has resulted in flagrant rashes of intolerance and related physical attacks.

Brown's history made him a very poor spokesman for a moral lifestyle and international political rhetoric. He is a convicted sex offender and spent time in federal prison for conspiracy to commit bank fraud. Between January 2002-November 2004, Brown and three other men were involved in a check kiting scheme. By his published admission, these crimes were designed to finance international terror and Jihadist activities.

Whether any of his murders were motivated strictly by his personal paranoia towards homosexuality will likely be determined in court. What is evident is that one deluded individual, presuming to be a follower of Islam, robbed four vibrant young men of their lives.

Nothing in the Koran rationalizes such senseless acts and an existence tainted by rampant criminality.

In May 2018, Ali Muhammad Brown received a life sentence without the possibility of parole for the murder of Brendan Tevlin. Brown's extradition to King County will eventually follow to stand trial for the three Washington homicides. A date has not been established for his transfer.

At his sentencing, Brown initially apologized to the parents and then raced to a rambling and nonsensical monologue that appeased no one in the courtroom. He repeatedly asked *to be treated as a human being, not a monster.*

The judge called Brendan Tevlin's murder *one of the most heinous, horrific, brutal crimes I have ever presided over.*

The audacity of Brown labeling his cold-blooded and

senseless murders a *domestic jihad* is as baseless as a credible monster or braying ass denying his identity.

Dwone Anderson and Ahmed Said Murder Location: 29th and South King, Seattle

James William Cushing: The Vulnerability of a Fractured Mind

In September 1990, shortly after his arrest for suspected murder, James William Cushing asked the investigating detective:

"Why didn't you arrest me sooner?"

Videotaped by the Seattle Police Department in connection with the March 13, 1990 stabbing of 63 year-old Geneva MacDonald, Cushing admitted to breaking into her Queen Anne neighborhood house. He volunteered during his interview that he had also hacked her to death with a pickax and her own sewing scissors.

Why?

He confessed that he was *out of control*.

The ax employed had been taken from a nearby back porch at a house Cushing had broken into four days earlier. The tool had been dusted for prints by the police and returned to the owner. The owner hadn't bothered to return the ax to its former concealed location. It laid out exposed to the elements. Cushing returned to the earlier break-in site and reclaimed his prize, which became the killing weapon employed on Geneva MacDonald. Traces of the police finger print dust remained on the handle at the crime scene.

Cushing, 36, was developmentally disabled with an extended history of mental illness. His primary concern during his police interview was that neither his mother nor therapist knew of his activities.

According to published reports, just prior to the attack on

March 13, Cushing was distraught after a security guard had hassled him at a nearby shopping mall. He returned to the familiar Queen Anne district where he spent much of his time walking the streets. He went looking purportedly to talk with someone in order to calm himself.

Instead, he entered MacDonald's multi-level house through an unlooked door and mounted a staircase into her bedroom. Upon entering, his mind went blank. His sole recollection was stabbing and cutting her to death. He was not acquainted with MacDonald. Afterwards, he lingered inside the house, eating Cheerios and a banana and laid down for a brief rest. He lifted $25 out of her purse and some jewelry from an upstairs drawer before departing for Tacoma.

Seattle's Queen Anne district is a sprawling and quaint neighborhood of Colonial and Craftsman styled houses. In 1990, security was often lax and doors or windows frequently unlocked. During that year, a pattern of disturbing and bizarre break-ins, most attributable to Cushing, involved transients entering homes, usually unoccupied and eating food left out. Theft rarely accompanied the visits.

Six months after the murder, a West Seattle apartment was broken into. The intruder, once again Cushing, left disturbing scrawls on the walls noting *The Killer Has Returned*. An ax was left at the foot of the staircase. This acknowledgement would later confirm the basis of his recognition that his acts were wrong.

A week later, he returned to the Queen Anne district with the intent of another break-in. This time, Cushing's evasive good fortune eluded him. The homeowner snapped a photo of him escaping the house via an Instamatic camera. The photo was submitted to police, who were aware of Cushing's identity and background.

During August 1990, he had been taken to a local Medical Center for psychiatric evaluation after he was observed screaming, threatening and brandishing a knife at a neighborhood park. Incredibly he was evaluated and released. There were too many James Cushing's types roaming Seattle and too few confined spaces to monitor them.

Once the police had his photo identification, apprehension required only a few days. His haunts and habits were well known including a Queen Anne tavern, the downtown rescue mission and the video section of a local record store. He was ultimately captured and arrested downtown.

Cushing's history included institutionalization on numerous occasions under supervised medical care. Based on his documented mental history, his trial focused primarily on his mental competence rather than guilt. No one disputed that he was a disturbed individual. Was he capable of distinguishing the immorality of his acts?

The voices he claimed that commanded him to kill may have served as a convenient ploy. They resembled severe schizophrenia. He admitted to considering suicide on multiple occasions after killing Geneva MacDonald, but never acted out on his guilt. Such admissions further indicated to the jury that he knew that his actions were wrong.

At the conclusion of his February 1991 trial, the jury was convinced that he was responsible for his actions. Despite his insanity plea, they convicted him of aggravated murder, first degree attempted murder and numerous breaking and entering charges. He was sentenced to life in prison without the possibility of parole. He is currently interned at the Monroe Correctional Complex after a stint at the Washington Corrections Center in Shelton.

Geneva MacDonald's killing was preventable had Cushing been institutionalized. The problem persists for society, however that isolating potentially violent personalities becomes both expensive and in many eyes, a direct violation of their civil rights.

Walking the sidewalks of any major urban center, the potential risk of violence is evident from similar individuals. Mental illness compounded by criminality does not respect geographical boundaries. There have been few effective or successful solutions that have adequately addressed the threat.

As long as the overpopulation of mental health facilities and depleted budgets remain, the problem will persist.

**Geneva McDonald Murder Site:
1611 Bigelow Avenue, Seattle**

John Alkins: Crossing Professional Boundaries Into Extremities

A freestanding brick fireplace, several mature pine trees and the remnants of a house foundation linger on a solitary lot bordering the Olympia Eld Inlet along Puget Sound. The secluded neighborhood features an assortment of multi-level and single-story residences, many dating back from the 1930's. The vacant space remains in austere contrast to the natural beauty inherent in the pristine location.

Amidst the natural beauty and serenity, the absence of a structure is puzzling. Why would such a prime location, especially considering the aggressive real estate market, remain available?

It was occupied by John Alkins, a 58-year-old counselor for the Washington State Behavioral Health Resources (BHR).

Atkins was employed by the BHR for twenty years. He was fired in December 2012 for violating the agency's policy concerning professional boundaries.

The counselor-patient relationship is tenuous. The therapist must be firmly but compassionately in control. The patient is absolutely dependent on their integrity and ability to separate clinical aid from personal urges. Trust and distance must be absolute. A sexual liaison between a counselor and their patient is clearly unethical.

Professional therapists are acutely aware of this prohibition. The American Counseling Association's code of published ethics mandate that sexual or romantic relationships are forbidden for a minimum of five years following final professional contact. Given the power dynamics of the two involved parties, it is dubious that crossing these boundaries is rarely if ever healthy for the patient.

John Alkins treated Lia Year Tricomo, thirty years his junior, while she was enrolled in a Pro 12 Step Behavioral Health program. Tricomo had a history of mental illness and violence. She had been convicted of assault, threatening her family and had attempted suicide.

Alkins had sustained contact with Tricomo after her treatment had concluded and his own job dismissal. He invited her to move in with him into his beachfront home. On April 29, 2013, she agreed. His motives and intentions became clear the following day.

The afternoon of April 30th began with the pair indulging in a bottle of Vodka. Tricomo was then enrolled in an Alcoholic Anonymous (AA) program for a drinking addiction. Their recreational imbibing moved upstairs into Alkins' master bedroom where he initiated sexual contact. She indicted his advances were unwanted, but she didn't forcibly discourage Alkins.

Lia Tricomo had her own agenda to fulfill.

Tricomo attempted to tie up Alkins. He refused. She abruptly slit his throat with a folding razor blade she'd previously hidden in the room. The cut wasn't fatal. According to newspaper accounts, Alkins walked around his house attempting to apply pressure and cease the bleeding. Tricomo trailed him and made certain he couldn't leave the premises. The excessive blood loss had weakened him. A struggle ensued near the front door of the residence. Tricomo was able to strangle him with an extension cord.

Newspapers reports indicated that he was discovered lying

face down on his bed with the cord still wrapped around his neck. There was a large pool of blood on the floor.

Tricomo remained in Alkins' house that evening and slept throughout the night. In the morning she checked on the cadaver and prepared breakfast. She attempted unsuccessfully to withdraw money online from his bank accounts. She drove Alkins' car to an AA meeting that evening where she confessed to the killing and asked for assistance. A member of the group took her to a local hospital's mental health ward. She was arrested for the murder.

In January 2015, Lia Tricomo was sentenced to over 35 years for a combination of second-degree murder, assault and stolen vehicle charges. She is currently interned at the Washington Corrections Center for Women in Gig Harbor.

The tragedy behind John Alkins' killing becomes more than a simple homicide. By knowingly and flagrantly violating his ethical standards with an emotionally imbalanced woman, he created a volatile environment resulting in tragedy.

Alkin's remaining family was devastated. The razed house and vacant lot exemplify the extreme consequences of his poor judgment.

**John Alkins Murder Site:
3814 Sunset Beach Drive NW, Olympia**

John Fiori: The Eruption and Rage of an Invisible Individual

John Fiori lived a lonely secluded existence in an apartment on the south slope of the Queen Anne district of Seattle. His neighbors knew little about him and he worked a night shift sorting mail at the main post office.

The 47-year-old Fiori was the sort of individual that seems invisible in an urban environment. He attracted little attention and kept his curtains routinely closed due to his late night employment.

He had never married, had no children and apparently few friends or notable female companions. On the evening of July 17, 1993, he picked up prostitute Alane Scott in front of an Aurora district motel, since demolished, and engaged her for sexual services in his apartment.

Scott, 28, was a mother of four and lived her own precarious existence. She had lost each of her children to the state due to negligence and her profession. She had an ongoing heroin addiction and numerous convictions for theft, prostitution and drug charges.

Once they completed their sexual liaison, Fiori decided to shower, unwisely leaving Scott unattended in his apartment. True to her instincts, she searched his sportscoat and located an envelop of cash. When he exited the bathroom and saw her rifling through the money, he exploded.

He grabbed a kitchen knife and stabbed her in the chest. He then strangled her. She miraculously survived his initial onslaught but only temporarily. She staggered to his door where he tackled her. He grabbed a gun from one of his drawers, put a pillow over her head to muffle the noise and pulled the trigger.

He left her soaking in his bathtub for over a day before deciding to dismember her with an axe. The disposal became problematic when he was pulled over in North Seattle the following evening for driving erratically. The body had already been distributed in multiple locations. Blood was evident on his hands, the steering wheel and outside of the trunk hatch. He claimed he had been cleaning fish. The police officer had no grounds to detain him, so he was released. The officer recorded his license plate number.

The following day, Scott's decapitated body was discovered nude in a quiet residential district. The police paid a visit to Fiori's apartment based on his suspicious stop from the night before. He casually invited them inside. The bloodstains were still evident on the carpet and his explanations and excuses defied logic. He was arrested and confessed to dumping the rest of Scott in a dumpster by Green Lake. The head and her extremities were never recovered. By the time detectives arrived to the dumpster, the contents were en route to a landfill in Oregon.

John Fiori pleaded guilty and received a 27-year prison sentence. His name no longer appears on the published State of Washington prison rolls. He may have successfully served out his term. Assuming this, he has likely assimilated back into society as simply another insignificant and forgotten individual who shared a brief instant of notoriety.

**John Fiori's Killing Site:
518 Prospect, Seattle**

Kyle Huff: The Capital Hill Massacre

No one attending a rave afterparty following the March 25, 2006 *Better Off Undead* concert in the southeastern Capitol Hill neighborhood of Seattle anticipated the event would be remembered in infamy.

The party was located in a residence approximately a mile away from the concert staged at the Capitol Hill Arts Center. Approximately 350 people attended the production including 28-year-old Kyle Huff. Huff was invited to the gathering that began at approximately 4:00 a.m.

He was unfamiliar with anyone at the party, but reportedly spoke pleasantly with several attendees. His behavior did not foreshadow the rampage that was to follow. At some point he left the gathering and strolled to his truck parked nearby.

From the cabin he removed two semi-automatic guns and over 300 pounds of ammunition. On his return, he symbolically spray painted *NOW* on the sidewalk and steps of a bordering house.

When he arrived at the party house, he immediately opened fire on five people who were talking together on the front steps and porch. He barged through the front door and shot two more people on the first level. He then mounted the staircase and blasted through the locked door of a bathroom where a couple had taken refuge. He missed both of them.

The shooting lasted five minutes. He was heard to announce *there's plenty for everyone*, assuming that he meant ammunition.

The Seattle police responded immediately and converged

towards the house. A nearby patrol officer had heard the shots and arrived on the scene at the conclusion of the shooting. Huff spotted him as he was descending the staircase. Before the officer could even issue a warning, Huff abruptly placed the gun in his mouth and shot himself through the head.

Police investigators found additional weaponry inside his truck but an absolute absence of a motive.

Huff shared an apartment with an identical twin brother in North Seattle, who was unaware of his brother's intent and activities. Nearly a month after the massacre, a handwritten letter surfaced attributed to Huff. The text provided a potential answer. The letter detailed Huff's alienation and disgust with the provocative and libertine lifestyle of habitual partygoers. It ended with a quotation *Now, Kids, Now*, consistent with his cryptic spray painted message. Some speculation contended that his message was lifted from a Nirvana song with a chorus refrain of *now, now, now, now*.

Whatever explanation proved accurate, Huff took his interpretation with him. Six people died in the rampage including Melissa Moore, Suzanne Thorne, Justin Schwartz, Christopher Williamson, Jeremy Martin and Jason Travers. They ranged in age between 14-32. Two other teenagers were seriously injured.

The loathsome, desperate act of Kyle Huff provided no fresh insight into the eternal adage of why misery must usually demands company.

**Kyle Huff Shooting Spree:
2112 East Republican, Seattle**

The Marysville-Pilchuck High School Shooting: A Familiar Scenario Targeted Towards Atypical Victims

The rash of American school shootings has often followed a disturbingly familiar pattern. In summary: a social outcast decides to revenge his tormentors or target a popular audience that he has been excluded from.

Jaylen Fryberg did not fit the prototype shooter profile, nor did the victims: his closest friends. On October 24, 2014, he texted these friends to an early meal at 10:35 a.m. in the school cafeteria. Their attendance in some cases meant skipping a scheduled class. Five responded and sat together at one table along with two other students. Approximately 150 students were in the lunchroom at the same time.

Shortly after his invitation, Fryberg group texted to members of his family and the families of his invited friends an apology for his impending actions, an explanation for his motives and detailed plans for his funeral.

At 10:39 a.m. he entered the cafeteria and sat down at a different table apart from his puzzled friends. He began verbally berating them. He then pulled out an automatic handgun from his backpack. He methodically fired at least eight shots exclusively at his friends. He fatally shot Zoe and Gia Soriano, Shaylee Chuckulnaskit and a cousin, Andrew Fryberg, all between the age of 14 and 15. He wounded three others.

He paused following his initial fuselage perhaps to reload. A first-year social studies teacher moved towards him to intervene. Fryberg made eye contact, but rather than adding her to the casualty list, he put the gun under his chin and pulled the trigger. He fell on top of the others.

Just minutes preceding the shooting, Fryberg had a tense exchange with his English teacher. The conflict was based on Fryberg being disrespectful to other students in the class and resting his head on his desk to look at his phone. His instructor chastised him twice. Each time Fryberg reached into his backpack with a menacing glare.

He hesitated. Instead of threatening the teacher, he decided that he had a larger perceived score to settle with his friends.

Fryberg was a 15-year-old freshman student who was considered *generally happy*. He participated on the school's football and wrestling team. He reportedly found his first year of high school a difficult adjustment as evidenced by failing grades and truancy.

His emotional imbalance was attributed to a recent break-up with a girlfriend who rejected him due to his violent tendencies. He had asked another girl, Zoe Galasso out for a date but was spurned because she was already dating his cousin, Andrew Fryberg. Both became victims of the shooting.

The shooting had been clearly planned in advance. It is difficult to know if any flagrant warning signals were overlooked. It is equally difficult to assume that someone was even paying attention.

In an unprecedented follow-up scenario, Fryberg's father was arrested five months later for purchasing nine weapons including the fatal handgun used in the shooting. He had lied on a background application check that would have prohibited him legally from making the purchases. In April 2015, a federal jury found him guilty of knowingly owning firearms that he legally could not possess. He is awaiting sentencing, which could imprison him for several years.

Jayson's ease of access to his firearms is merely one outrage that haunts this tragedy. The weapon was kept in his father's pickup. Marysville-Pilchuck High School did not employ metal detectors at their entrance doors, a sad reality many public high schools have been compelled to implement. Gun rights proponents still do not concur with the obvious conclusion that guns and educational institutions are an incompatible combination.

In the aftermath of seeking a cohesive motive as to why a 15-year-old would harm exclusively his friends, Fryberg's text message was succinct. He typed that he didn't want to *go alone*.

With a mass shooting, the victims far outnumber the actual physical dead. Fryberg became responsible for his closest friend's deaths but also an entire student body, faculty, numerous families and a community that will be forever traumatized by his narcissistic actions. Marysville High relocated the cafeteria to another section of the campus.

**Marysville/Pilchuck High School Cafeteria Shooting:
5611 108th Street NE, Marysville**

Michael Harmon: A Contender In The Dumbest Homicide Possible Competition

Edward Weed, 46, reportedly first encountered Michael Harmon, 32, in 2008 while incarcerated for driving under the influence. Shortly after his release, Harmon began habitually hanging around Weed's North Spokane residence. According to Weed's mother, he stopped associating with him shortly afterwards when Harmon stole from him. Harmon, however, proved himself a troublesome dependent to evade.

The pair had a volatile relationship for the next six years. During this period, Harmon accrued seven diverse misdemeanor domestic violence convictions for assault and violating protection and no-contact orders. In September 2012, he pleaded guilty to a felony domestic violence charge in a case not involving Weed.

On October 29, 2014, Harmon returned to Weed's residence for undisclosed reasons. They had a physical altercation where he punched Weed in the face multiple times rendering him unconscious. He suffered a fractured nose and cuts on his forehead and cheek. These injuries would not have been life threatening. Weed collapsed onto a couch. Harmon strangled him and banged his head on the ground prompting a seizure that stopped his breathing.

Harmon proceeded to steal his phone, several packs of cigarettes and various household items. He left the house in disarray and trashed the bedroom. He stabbed Weed's dog Tasha in the face and locked her in the bathroom.

Harmon returned to the house on November 3rd presumably to determine if he'd overlooked any additional items to steal. He bagged an Xbox, toilet paper and other items, which he then left in the house intending to return and retrieve later. He told authorities upon his arrest that he found Weed in the identical position on the couch with the addition of *black hands*. Harmon, during the same confession, confided to police that he *believed* Weed was dead but didn't want to call 911.

Weed's decomposing body was officially discovered on November 6th, eight days following the fatal assault by his mother. She was worried when he hadn't been returning her calls. Miraculously, his dog survived the ordeal in spite of multiple injuries and dehydration.

The incredulous Harmon returned to the house one final time on November 8th, to retrieve his haul and perhaps scour the premises one last time. A neighbor recognized him when he offered to rake her leaves. She telephoned police and Harmon was arrested the same day. He had apparently not considered flight as an option, even after the body had been discovered by authorities and removed.

Harmon was sentenced to 17 years in prison and is currently incarcerated at the Airway Heights Corrections Center where his long-term accommodation problem appears to be resolved.

**Edward Weed's Murder Site:
5418 N. Ash Street, Spokane**

A Street Culture Slaying Resembling A Traditional Murder

Theirs is a world that lingers on the outskirts of respectability. They are determined to never re-enter what they have previously rejected. Theirs is a lifestyle outside the boundaries of traditional laws. They create their own set of social mores and rules.

Periodically the street culture of young runaways cross boundaries and conflict with organized society. Olympia is considered one of Washington's safest and most tolerant communities. However, a culture of young adults and teenagers inhabit temporary homeless camps on the eastside, adjacent to Interstate 5 and hidden by sprawling wild blackberry bramble. Other temporary camps exist under protective overpasses or bridge spans.

The encampments are usually trashlined and the concrete freeway pilings often graffiti laden. During the daytime, many of the occupants panhandle in the city or simply lounge awaiting nightfall or their next hallucination. It is a pathetic and self-destructive lifestyle often accompanied by mental illness. Alcohol abuse and drug use is rampant, whether it is cannabis, meth or more expensive heroin.

In Thurston County, more than one-third of the homeless are 25 or younger and those numbers are likely underestimated.

Would they return to a *normal* environment if their families welcomed them back?

Many are adamant that their *true* families are not their biological families, but rather the friends and acquaintances they've accumulated while living on the fringe. Many claim the abuse and neglect they've suffered from their birth families are the very reason they left for the streets in the first place.

There are numerous community-funded agencies that provide them temporary shelter year round, but sadly too few beds accommodate too many bodies. The shelter, showers and meals are only temporary reprieves from the harsh and grinding outdoor elements. Most of these programs demand behavioral expectations that these potential tenants are unwilling to adhere to.

Olympia is merely a microcosm of a global problem where premature fatalities are not uncommon.

During October 2012, 19-year-old Christopher *Skitzo* Harrison stabbed 17 year-old Forest *Sonic* Bailey to death. The exact date has been as difficult to determine as his motive. The murder might have gone unheeded had not an inmate in the Nisqually Jail informed on Harrison. Passing on hearsay evidence, Harrison apparently had either confided to someone or bragged about the murder. The story circulated within the transient community.

After killing Bailey, Harrison recruited Eric *Discord* Davidson and Cammron *Red* Wallen to assist in burning the body. The two complied after stealing a metal barrel. They burned the remains over an entire evening. An unidentified female was present as an observer. She would later provide damaging testimony against the trio and was not charged as an accomplice.

After receiving the jail informant's tip, police located the burned remains. They expediently arrested Harrison as their prime suspect and Davidson and Wallen as accomplices.

In a detailed follow-up media interview with an individual who claimed friendship with all of the parties a year after the killing, curious language was used to describe the values shared between members of the homeless encampment. The most prominent included *trust*, *alliances* and *family*. The words seemed contradictory for members that would willingly burn the body of one of their own.

Leading up to their October 2014 trial, the bonds of group fidelity began to fray. Eric Davidson was the first to accept a plea bargain deal and proved very cooperative with police in filling in the details and events surrounding Bailey's death. He later expressed great remorse for his role in the cover-up.

Harrison maintained his defiant innocence until the mounting evidence and witnesses against him proved overwhelming. He altered his stance to confess that one evening he found Bailey raping two women in his tent. He then admitted to striking Bailey with a piece of wood and stabbing him in the abdomen three times. The two potential rape victims fled. They were never located to corroborate his improbable tale.

During his trial in October 2014, Harrison pleaded guilty to second-degree murder and was sentenced to 18 years and four months in prison. He is interned at the Coyote Ridge Corrections Center after a stint at the Clallam Bay Corrections Center. Wallen pleaded guilty to first-degree criminal assistance and received a two year and five month prison sentence. He is interned at the Stafford Creek Corrections Center after a stint at the Airway Heights Corrections Center. Davidson pleaded guilty to first-degree criminal assistance and received a reduced six-month sentence, which he has served to completion.

In the end, the perpetrators acted consistently in the manner of mainstream felons. Most exhibited the identical defiance, sentence negotiation tactics and public apologies *once* they were apprehended and faced conviction. All pretense of rejecting mainstream society or living differently or better vanished. Their ideology and culture appeared as empty as their ambitions beyond simple survival at public expense.

This apathy becomes the biggest challenge towards eradicating such a vicious cycle and pattern of self-destruction. A high percentage of the most affected will do little or nothing to change their own circumstances and prospects. They remain a society's burden that loathes their benefactor.

Olympia Homeless Camp Entrance

The Red Barn Door Tavern Massacre: The Reformation of A Vicious Mass Killer?

The roadway along International Boulevard in SeaTac has been the source for numerous abductions and homicides by some of Washington's most vicious serial killers.

No murder has haunted this boulevard of ghosts and demons more than the June 12, 1980 massacre at the Barn Door Tavern. Five people were attacked and robbed shortly before closing time. The night manager, Loran Dowell, bartender Robert Pierre and his girlfriend Linda Burford were savagely killed.

Dowell and Pierce were tied up inside the walk-in freezer and slaughtered execution style. Burford was raped, left nude and hanging by her neck from a railing. Two of the survivors were chocked with electrical cords around their necks and left for dead in the woman's bathroom.

The culprits, Timothy Pauley and Scott Smith were apprehended within hours of their savagery. Pauley pled guilty to three counts of murder and was sentence to three life terms. Scott was convicted to five life terms for the three murder counts and two assault counts.

Most observers would assume that justice had been served by the sentencing and the two captive animals would no longer be a threat to the state of Washington or humanity in general. Both were spared the death penalty when at the time of their conviction, capital punishment was briefly abolished.

Over thirty-five years later, both men remain alive and incarcerated. Smith is interned at the Stafford Creek Corrections Center State Penitentiary in Walla Walla and

Pauley at the Monroe Correctional Complex.

The Washington Indeterminate Sentencing Review Board reduced Pauley's minimum term on the last criminal count served making him eligible for parole in February 2018. Their decision was based on his declared remorse and behavior while incarcerated. The Chairperson of that body was quoted as acknowledging that Pauley *has been doing very, very well in prison.* Pauley's mentoring of other offenders, volunteering for inmate committees and avoiding serious infractions since 1995 qualified this observation.

None of the law enforcement investigators, surviving victims, their families, and legal prosecution team are in agreement with the decision. One of the original King County sheriff's homicide detectives, Dave Reichert, became a United States Congressman.

The essential question our legal system must address on a daily basis is whether prison compliance and behavior really matters with life stealing capital offenses. When the language of a sentence clearly states *life imprisonment*, are the terms addressing the life of a rodent, canine, or human being? Life imprisonment for older convictions sometimes does not become that.

While many lifetime incarcerated prisoners die of illness, old age or suicide, a percentage of lifers have actually been released back into society. Is society better off?

In the summary comments accompanying the Sentencing Review Board's decision, the chairperson noted that it is always pleasing to the board when people are different than who they were 30 years ago. People can and do change.

The current Washington governor may ultimately rescind the early release date. Whether habitually incarcerated individuals can and do change is interpretive. One fact is certain. Victims of murder have no option to evolve.

In 2016, Pauley went before his parole board hoping for a more expedited release date. Instead the parole board added an additional twenty-two years to his sentence. The circus continued when an appeals court overturned that decision and a new hearing was scheduled for late 2019. At that hearing, Pauley was denied parole.

**Red Barn Door Tavern Massacre:
14835 International Boulevard, Tukwila**

Aaron Ybarra: A School Shooting Prefaced By A Living Hell

Aaron Ybarra, 26 had an unusual fascination and admiration for the perpetrators of the 1999 Columbine High School massacre. He physically traveled to visit the scene of the killings in Colorado. Perhaps he envied their notoriety and wished empowerment for his own failing life.

His family upbringing was turbulent and patterned after a father with an excessive alcohol problem. Father and son were habitual drinking buddies. They shared a weaponry passion and residence stocked with eight handguns and rifles. This toxic mixology would frame a prelude to Ybarra's own aborted grasp at infamy.

In 2012, Aaron, not his father, began seeking help for his alcohol dependency. He met weekly with a therapist in a futile attempt to deal with his obsessive-compulsive disorder. He kept drinking. His counselor recommended a residential treatment facility to free him from his family environment. An assigned psychiatrist diagnosed the antipsychotic drug Risperdal to calm the multiple disturbing voices within in his head.

This combination of alcoholism, unhealthy family dependency and probable schizophrenia served as the building blocks and flagrant warning signs towards his ultimate disintegration. Only a two-year waiting period remained before detonation.

The damage to Aaron Ybarra was too pronounced and far along for effective treatment and therapy. In October 2012, police found him sprawled in the middle of the street outside his family home. He was drunk, depressed and despondent. Instead of committing him to an institution for evaluation, he was return to his unstable Mountlake Terrace home.

The police returned within the week to quell a drunken and menacing disturbance involving his father. His struggles with drug and alcoholism had resulted in five drunk-driving convictions. Aaron's younger brother had developed a heroin addiction. Theirs was a family teetering on the edge.

Both brothers had developed a youthful fascination towards firearms. Aaron worked for several years at a local gun range. His mother had enabled their obsession by registering the guns in her name when the boys were too young to legally purchase them.

The sum of this predictable destiny surfaced around 3:30 p.m. on the next to last afternoon of the 2014 academic spring semester. The shooting site was the foyer of Otto Miller Hall at Seattle Pacific University. He was unfamiliar with the campus and selected a two-story building housing computer science, engineering, physics and science education classrooms. His stated goal was to kill a maximum number of people.

Ybarra entered the ground floor armed with fifty rounds of ammunition and a hunting knife. He expected to die following the siege.

His pompous ambitions were thwarted shortly after he opened fire and killed student Paul Lee, 19 and wounding two other students. He was courageously pepper-sprayed while reloading and tackled by a student building monitor. Other students and faculty members arrived to pin him immobile. He had failed in his aspirations to create a major spectacle.

He was convicted in November of premeditated first-degree murder, three counts of attempted first-degree murder and one count of second-degree assault in November 2017. He was sentenced to 112 years in prison. He is currently interned at the Washington State Penitentiary in Walla Walla.

It is valid that heinous upbringing is instrumental in contributing towards the wreckage of a young and impressionable personality. Clearly his father proved an abysmal example. His mother is now deceased.

Aaron Ybarra, the adult, attempted to gain a sliver of notoriety to compensate for the failure he had become. His too late apology during sentencing rang empty, particularly since immediately after the shooting he was quoted as saying he had no sympathy for the victims.

If jailing incompetent parents was sufficient for eliminating crime and violent monsters, neither penal institutions nor the expanses of hell could accommodate the fresh influx. For now, atrocious abuse and neglect creates a purgatory for children that society ultimately pays the tariff for.

Seattle Pacific University Shooting:
Otto Miller Hall Foyer, 3469 3rd Avenue West, Seattle

The Man of A Thousand Identities

At 66, Turid *Turi* Bentley had finally found the man of her dreams or at least for the moment. John Williams had moved into her comfortable Gig Harbor residence in March 2006. The townhouse, formerly owned by her mother, is a two-block stroll from the southern Puget Sound shoreline. She originally met Williams through her activities selling vitamin products through the Mannatech networking company.

Williams, 62 described himself as a naturopathic doctor. Bentley's family and friends assumed that he was retired since he didn't work. The couple appeared to be married having gone through a ceremony but lacked a license to solemnize the union.

There were varied opinions expressed about John Williams. Bentley's adult son typified him as *odd, but nice enough*. He indicted that some family members were concerned about his financial motives regarding his mother. One of Bentley's long-time friends called her *a good person taken in by an evil man*. This same friend added that Williams had isolated her from family and friends during the year they'd known each other. Many neighbors expressed simple ignorance about even knowing Williams.

Seemingly without warning on March 29, 2007, the couple violently argued and Williams shot Turi Bentley to death. He also wounded an intervening neighbor critically Finally he turned the gun on himself and terminated what appeared to be a conventional murder-suicide.

At this climax, the sham of his life began to publicly unravel.

John Williams was not his actual name. Investigators, while combing through the crime scene discovered a locked container in the home attic. Inside were multiple identification cards with his picture, but a variety of alias. Some official IDs originated from diverse destinations such as the Virgin Islands and West Indies. The most revealing identifications traced him back to southern Oregon.

So who was John Williams?

The closest confirmed identity proved to be John William Branden, a former resident of Gold Beach, Oregon near the California border. In 1999, he was accused of tying up and raping his live-in girlfriend. He threatened to slice her up. He threatened to dispose of her body in the adjacent Pacific Ocean. She was able to escape her potential homicide and called police from a neighbor's home.

Branden fled before police arrived. He wasn't finished with his torment. He reportedly continued to taunt and threaten her by telephone. She disappeared into seclusion quite aware that his threats were valid.

Gold Beach Police issued arrest warrants for John William Branden for kidnapping, sexual assault, attempted murder and unlawful flight. He evaporated for over six years before encountering Turi Bentley. Doubtlessly other women became ensnared in his schemes during this period.

Police speculated that Braden intended to swindle Bentley out of her life's savings. This speculation may have triggered their fatal dispute. Although deeply religious, Turi was not likely a lovestruck imbecile. She had been married previously and had one son, two daughters, ten grandchildren and one great-grandchild.

It is likely that prior to her murder, she may have finally seen through Williams' manipulation and deceit. A confrontation may have provoked her murder. What is less evident is why a con artist such as John William Branden committed suicide.

The story seemed too surreal to avoid closer examination. In 2008, true crime author Ann Rule profiled the Bentley killing in her book *Mortal Danger* under the title *Till Death Do Us Part*.

Gig Harbor remains a tranquil suburban oasis, but periodically is vulnerable to respectable resembling serpents like John William Branden.

**Turid Bentley's Murder Site:
6876 Windlass Lane, Gig Harbor**

Jennifer Hopper: Devine Forgiveness for an Unpardonable Act

At approximately 3 a.m. on July 19, 2009, Isaiah Kalebu crawled through an open window of Teresa Butz and Jennifer Hopper's South Park district house. He violently taunted, raped, tortured and stabbed both women during a 90-minute ordeal.

Butz was fatally punctured through the heart and died on the street in front of her house. She had thrown a table through a bedroom window and pushed herself outside in a futile attempt to escape. Hopper struggled valiantly with her assailant despite receiving slash wounds on her neck and arms. She was able to flee through the gaping hole left by Butz.

Kalebu was apprehended within a week and tried two years later. He was convicted and sentenced to life in prison without the possibility of parole. He is currently incarcerated at the Monroe Correctional Complex after a stint at the Clallam Bay Corrections Center.

Kalebu stated at his trial that he was following *God's instructions* by attacking the two women. He appeared unrepentant for his actions and ranted viciously against the women's sexual orientation and relationship. He was strapped down in a restraint chair during the trial in response to his behavior. He had an extended history of mental illness.

Survivor Jennifer Hopper, by contrast offered a more concrete example of following God's instructions.

Butz and Hopper were domestic partners reportedly two months away from solemnizing their relationship officially with marriage banns.

The substance of Hopper's story is not simply about subsisting after a vicious and unjustifiable murder by a remorseless killer. She publicly forgave Kalebu at his trial and consistently continues to through numerous subsequently published articles. Divine and undeserved mercy is an example that illuminates profoundly amidst the blackest of evils. Most of us could not forgive a killer that had stolen the life of our closest intimate and forever altered our own life.

Jennifer Hopper was not only capable, but did so absent of piety.

The South Park neighborhood where the women lived will never be mistaken for Seattle's most elite quarter. The houses are wedged together tightly and appear foreboding during the daylight. The environment worsens during the darkness. Closely following Butz's murder, neighbors converged to assist and console. Some patrolled the streets with baseball bats, knives and guns searching for the perpetrator. It was a response you wouldn't observe in most affluent neighborhoods anywhere following a home invasion.

Five days later, police released a surveillance video of a suspect with a pitbull trying to break into the City Hall building in nearby Auburn. A bus driver spotted Kalebu and his dog near Seattle's Magnuson Park following the distribution of widely circulating wanted posters. The killer was arrested shortly afterwards.

Sometimes the purist examples of humanity originate from the humblest of circumstances. A disreputable neighborhood arose in an attempt to protect and avenge one of their own. A woman, who had lost her life partner, could exonerate a murderer who despised what she represented. Symbols of true community are not always exampled by statuary, public proclamations or real estate values.

Isaiah Kalebu did not merit Jennifer Hopper's forgiveness by his actions. He was freely offered the gift because she didn't allow revenge and hatred to become her dominant response.

**Teresa Butz and Jennifer Hopper Rape and Murder Site:
727 S. Rose Drive, Seattle**

Zachary Craven: The Devalued Exchange of Human Life

The value of a human life seemed momentarily contained within the contents of a ceramic piggy bank through the desperate eyes of 24-year-old Zachary Craven.

Craven began July 7, 2015 by murdering his grandmother, 66-year-old Angelika Hayden in Skyway. He had formerly lived with her until his threatening actions of September 14, 2014. On that day, he had dangerously jerked on the steering wheel of her car while she was driving him to a hospital to acquire pain medication.

Hayden had a history of trying to protect Craven from incarceration. She was terrified of him, but also felt pity for him. Craven rewarded her fidelity by stabbing her cat, threatening to kill her dog and committing a sequence of physical assaults. His personality was in the process of unraveling and she overlooked the obvious extreme signs until it became too late. Perhaps she sensed that he was simply a victim of parental neglect and still redeemable.

After the 2014 threat to his grandmother, Craven roomed with her close friend in Kent.

Two weeks before Hayden's death, Craven was convicted of charges from the previous year. The counts were domestic violence and felony harassment for threatening to kill his grandmother. He was ordered to undergo drug treatment in lieu of a prison sentence and was issued a no-contact order for Hayden. He urgently needed money and was nearing detonation.

Five days before his grandmother's murder, he assaulted his housing host by pistol-whipping him. The same day, he failed to report to his initial drug treatment appointment. Three days later, he ignored the no contact rule with his grandmother by visiting her house to retrieve some belongings. He appeared intoxicated and made demands for money. She telephoned police.

On a Tuesday morning, he executed Hayden with a bullet to the head. Lacking funds and a hideaway destination, his escape prospects were limited.

Hours afterwards, he visited the residence of a former girlfriend who he had dated for three and a half years previously. She lived with her family in Renton. He had exhibited a pattern of threatening behavior and physical abuse in the past towards her. He was unaware the family was on vacation with their daughter. Her friend, Meagan Smith was housesitting the property during their trip.

Smith answered the door. Neither of them was well acquainted. Craven demanded the contents of a piggy bank that he claimed was half his property. She reportedly brought it to him laying it on a counter. In exiting, he neglected to take it with him. What followed was a puzzling act. Craven also shot her and the family's elderly dog to death in the head. Nothing else in the house was apparently removed.

Meagan Smith failed to pick up the family at the airport that night as was previously arranged. The family taxied home around midnight and discovered her body. While police were interviewing Craven's ex-girlfriend, he telephoned. He asked her to meet him alone at a nearby drug store. He confessed that he was in trouble, but didn't elaborate.

She avoided a probable death rendezvous. Police apprehend him and took him into custody.

Zachary Craven was sentenced to 72 years in prison in August 2018 after a jury found him guilty of two counts of first-degree murder and second-degree assault for the earlier pistol whipping. He is currently incarcerated at the Washington State Penitentiary in Walla Walla.

Angelika Hayden Murder Site:
11023 Park View Avenue S, Bryn Mawr-Skyway

Meagan Smith Murder Site: 2024 SE 17th Court, Renton

The Anderson Family Killings: Three Generations Lost on Christmas Eve

Wayne and Judy Anderson lived in an isolated hillside residence on the wooded outskirts of rural Carnation, 25 miles east of Seattle. Their house was located at the crest of a serpentine roadway, seemingly unwelcome by prevalent signage to outsiders and curious visitors.

Wayne, 60 was a Boeing engineer and Judy, 61 was a local postal worker. They had two children. Their oldest son, Scott, 30 was married to Erica, 32 with two offspring Olivia, 6 and Nathan, 3. Wayne and Judy's youngest daughter, Michele, 29, lived adjacent to their house in a mobile home with her boyfriend Joseph McEnroe, also 29.

On December 24, 2007, Judy Anderson was preparing for a family gathering and in the process of wrapping presents. Unanticipated by her or Wayne, daughter Michele and Joseph McEnroe arrived early and armed with grievances to resolve.

Michele nursed a simmering grudge that she had been slighted and mistreated by her parents and brother throughout her life. She felt her perceived inferior status and disregard by her family intolerable. Disputes, bitterness and resentment had festered for too long in her mind. Christmas Eve would prove the climax for resolution.

In a later confession, she pinpointed three major grievances. First, her brother Scott owed her money. Additionally, he had reneged on a promise to repair her car the previous year. Finally, she felt undue pressure from her family to pay rent for living in their trailer on their property.

Her fury ignited. She fired a pistol at her father wounding him. The gun jammed. Her partner, McEnroe completed the execution and then killed her mother. The pair relocated both bodies into a backyard shed behind the house. They covered each body with cardboard. They meticulously reorganized the house.

Anderson and McEnroe waited for her brother and his family to arrive.

Upon their arrival, the foursome settled into the household presumably awaiting Wayne and Judy's appearance. Michele then shot her brother to death. In the subsequent mayhem, McEnroe mercilessly killed Erica Anderson and her two children attempting to flee because he didn't want witnesses. The bodies lay sprawled in the house for the next two days.

A postal co-worker of Judy's discovered the carnage upon visiting the house. Judy's failure to appear at work was uncharacteristic. The police were telephoned. While local detectives were surveying the crime scene, Michelle Anderson and Joseph McEnroe drove up to their trailer. They were interrogated and arrested immediately. Their guilt was as evident as their lack of preparation for a planned escape.

They had neither destination nor financial resources to take flight. They both pled guilty. Their trial merely resolved the elemental question as to whether they deserved to continue living following such a heinous act.

During their 2015 trial, McEnroe blamed Anderson for provoking his involvement. She agreed and accepted full responsibility. McEnroe's lawyers blamed his susceptibility to coercion on personal struggles with mental illness, a chaotic upbringing and *fragile* mental state.

The question of his mental stupidity became evident when McEnroe admitted to softening his voice during courtroom testimony to simulate a more pleasant sound. Michele offered meager remorse between flowing tears except that both of them felt really bad and she should have walked away from it. Her parents, brother and his family were unable to accept her apology.

The couple was convicted of first-degree murder on all six counts and both sentenced to life in prison. Michele Anderson is currently interned at the Washington Corrections Center for Women in Gig Harbor after a stint at the Women's Center in Belfair and Joseph McEnroe is imprisoned at the Washington State Penitentiary in Walla Walla.

There are often few effective remedies for a family member who resents their perceived role as the least-favored child. Violence is an extreme but often sadly reoccurring solution. With the Anderson family, the sensed outrage obliterated three generations within a single holiday afternoon.

**Anderson Family Murder Site:
1806 346th Avenue NE, Carnation**

The Charles Goldmark Family Murder: Erroneous Presumptions

The polarization of political rhetoric has created extremities often lacking empathy, concrete rationale and accuracy. Simplistic presumptions are established regarding points of view based on casual research that result in extreme consequences.

A drifter and member of an extreme-conservative political group, David Lewis Rice presumed that civil litigation attorney Charles Goldmark was both Jewish and Communist. He arrived at his conclusions based on a Seattle newspaper article he had read in March 1983.

The article confirmed neither fact. It simply noted Charles Goldmark's prominence within the Democratic Party and that his family had just moved into a residence in the upscale Madrone district. The text provided Rice with a residential address.

For two years, Rice planned to eliminate Charles and Annie Goldmark. In a later confession, he indicated that he had stalked their residence on two previous occasions within the six months prior to hatching his plan of action.

He had delusionally targeted the Goldmarks. They were neither Jewish nor communists. His expressed aim was both political and financial. He assumed that large deposits of cash would be hidden in the house. He was completely unaware that the Goldmark's had two young sons, Colin and Derek.

During the early evening of December 26, 1985, Rice transferred to their residence by city bus. He was armed with a toy pistol, handcuffs, two bottles of chloroform, two rags and wore a concealing green parka. He gained entry into the house pretending to be a deliveryman.

Once admitted, he managed to bind the four family members, chloroformed them into unconsciousness, and then beat them with a steam iron. He stabbed the couple to death. The killings required approximately 25 minutes and David Rice escaped into the night. His clothing was stained in blood, so he walked back to his residence rather than return by bus. A report indicated that he actually returned to the crime scene an hour later trying to retrieve the handcuffs he'd mistakenly left. By the time he arrived, police had already cordoned off the house.

The same evening, Rice slept at an acquaintance's house. His host was unaware about the news of the brutal killings. The killer penned a confessional note on the kitchen table before both men slept. That morning, his acquaintance read the note and discovered while going out for coffee about the killings. He telephoned police, who arrested Rice as he was hastily exiting the apartment.

Despite his erroneous choice of victims, Rice expressed only remorse for killing the Goldmark's two sons. Both did not expire immediately from their injuries. Within two weeks, both died.

At Rice's trial in 1986, he pleaded insanity while repeatedly displaying psychotic symptoms throughout the proceedings. His actions did not impress the jury. He was expediently convicted on four counts of first-degree murder and sentenced to death. The conviction was later overturned due to the ineptitude of his legal representation. He was re-tried and convicted in 1998. He pleaded guilty in exchange for a life sentence. He is currently imprisoned at the Washington State Penitentiary in Walla Walla.

Political discussion and rhetoric today frequently cross inflammatory boundaries. Tolerance and acceptance of alternative viewpoints often seem abandoned. Leaders become demonized. When erroneous propaganda incites murder, responsibility seems notably absent from the rhetorical sources and their representatives.

**Charles Goldmark Family Murder Site:
724 36th Avenue, Seattle**

Barrett Bailey: Vanished and Renamed But Never Too Far Removed From Suspicion

One may change an identity, but ultimately in the age of forensics, one cannot entirely vanish from their past.

On February 16, 1997, Deborah Bailey, 32, was found shot four times in the head as she sat in her Volkswagen convertible alongside the remote Naches-Wenas grade outside of Naches. The obvious suspect became her husband, Barrett Bailey, who had reported her missing the same evening.

The couple had been married 3 1/2 contentious years and she reportedly confided to friends about physical and emotional abuse. They had two children together and rumors circulated that she was contemplating divorce and obtaining custody of their sons.

Barrett Bailey claimed that Deborah had a severe cocaine habit and was probably killed by one of her dealers whom she owed money. Deborah's family denied viewing any signs of her drug use.

Character conjectures became difficult to substantiate.

The police never wavered on their suspicion of Barrett Bailey as their prime suspect. They lacked evidence to indict. They waited. Bailey wanted the convertible returned. The police department refused, asserting it as crucial evidence to the case. In 2000, he was paid $15,000 for the car. Within months after the murder, he was convicted on possession of stolen property after stolen car parts were found in his home during an investigative search.

Two year later, his home in Selah burned down. His insurance company rejected his claim citing that the fire was intentionally set.

Bailey changed his name to Barry Beckford and relocated to Priest River, Idaho, north of Coeur d'Alene.

A January 2015 episode of the television program *Cold Justice* aired the case. The show outlined the investigation into Debbie Bailey's killing highlighting several circumstantial clues. The three suspicious indicators included a telephone record of a call made by Bailey to a friend and suspected drug dealer on the evening of February 15. Deborah Bailey's purse lay undisturbed on the car's back seat indicating that she probably had been a front seat passenger. A former co-worker indicated on camera that Barrett Bailey had dismantled and disposed of a .22-caliber pistol (same at the murder weapon) into a nearby river. Bailey had further expressed remorse to him over an act that his associate assumed to be his wife's murder. The disposal and conversation were denied by Bailey to have ever taken place.

Investigators indicated that Barrett Bailey and his friend could find no one to verify their whereabouts on the evening of the killing. Police speculated that both men may have accompanied Deborah to the murder location or rendezvoused at the scene.

Whether these conclusions are accurate or simply a desperate attempt to solve a lingering cold case, Barry Beckford will be judged in court. The nightmare of suspicion he cited in his own television interview will have to be proven. With constitutional protection against double jeopardy, the prosecution will need to conclusively substantiate a 20-year-old case before a jury.

On January 22, 2015, Barry Beckford was officially arrested for the murder of his wife. He waved extradition in Idaho and stood trial. In March 2015, prosecutors added two counts of witness tampering after he attempted to influence the statements of his two sons concerning the murder case.

In May 2017, in one of the strangest sentencing cases imaginable, Beckford entered an *Alford plea* under a deal struck with prosecutors following a deadlocked jury in his first-degree murder trial the month before. The Alford plea allowed Beckford to continue asserting his innocence, while admitting the prosecution had enough evidence to persuade a jury in a potential trial to find him guilty.

The second-degree manslaughter along with two charges of witness tampering conviction resulted in sentencing of 27 months in jail. As he had already spent 28 months incarcerated while awaiting trial. He was released almost immediately following the verdict. He returned to Idaho where he was originally taken into custody doubtlessly proclaiming his triumph and innocence. Justice remains elusive in the shooting death of Deborah Bailey on an isolated stretch of Naches-Wenas.

**Deborah Bailey's Murder Site:
Naches Wenas Road, Naches**

The Murder Experiment that Concluded Dreadfully Wrong

On August 31, 2012, Yancy Knoll, 43 steered his red Subaru SUV to the intersection of Seattle's 15th Avenue Northeast and Northeast 75th Street just north of the Roosevelt Reservoir in the right lane. Knoll had worked in the wine and restaurant industries for many years and was currently employed by the QFC grocery chain as a wine steward.

While waiting at the stoplight, a silver BMW Z4 convertible pulled up alongside in the center lane. Within seconds, the driver opened fire on Knoll five times. The gunfire shattered the BMW's passenger side window and struck Knoll three times in the head killing him instantly.

The killer sped off at high speed, veering into an oncoming lane and ran a red light. He launched his vehicle at the top of a steep hill landing loudly at the bottom. The car then disappeared into a residential neighborhood. Surveillance cameras at the reservoir captured footage of the speeding convertible.

Knoll slumped over the steering wheel with his hands firmly attached. There had been no advanced warning to his abrupt demise. A 9-mm casing was found adjacent to his car, one was located in the dashboard and a fifth shot exited a window and was located inside a nearby house.

Initially no one could fathom a motive for the random shooting. A composite sketch abstracted from eyewitnesses detailed the shooter's appearance. A tip within the first month led investigators to Dinh Bowman, a former child prodigy who had taken university computer classes at the age of 13. Currently, Bowman was employed as an engineer at Vague Industries, a South Seattle based robotics shop.

Bowman lived only ten blocks from the shooting site. Police began staking out his house. With a search warrant, they located the silver BMW Z4 in his garage. The passenger side window had been evidently replaced and new tires installed. Investigators confiscated his computers. At trial, online browsing records and hundreds of saved files would construct a detailed portrait of Bowman's research prior to the shooting and aftermath interest.

Within the Bowman residence, detectives discovered a *gun room* set up to accommodate his obsession with firearms. The facility included long rifles, scopes and bullet-making equipment. Two empty 9-mm holsters were confiscated but no handguns.

Follow-up research traced the window replacement to a dealership in Portland, Oregon where he paid cash under an alias. The fresh tires were bought from a tire shop in nearby Lynnwood. Employees noted that Bowman and his wife struggled to load the four new tires and four used tires into her small Mercedes-Benz. They also observed only minimal wear on the used tires and the distinctive white rims had been spray-painted black.

These four tires were located at the Vague Industries South Seattle warehouse. Their treads matched the skid marks at the shooting scene. A slide for a 9-mm handgun was also found concealed in a plastic container, wrapped in paper towels and placed on a shelf in the back of the shop.

At Bowman's trial, a disturbing profile emerged enabling prosecutors to label him a *student of murder*. Bowman spent hours studying forensics evidence, gunpowder residue and assassination tactics enabling the perfect murder and most importantly, *getting away with it*. His computers became a reference resource with hundreds of related articles. Videos of Bowman at a shooting range and evasive driving course verified his proficiency with firearms and speeding vehicles.

On the day of the murder, Bowman had turned off his cell phone to avoid any potential tracking evidence. Two hours following the killing, he shared dinner with his wife at a *Red Robin* restaurant.

As his prospects worsened at trial, Bowman adopted two unorthodox but noteworthy tactics. The first was to alter his physical appearance and hairstyle. He modified his cocky urban professional persona during his original interrogations into a meek and passive schoolboy appearance.

His second tactic utterly backfired. Bowman *admitted* shooting Knoll. He claimed himself the actual victim and the shooting became self-defense motivated by Knoll's road rage. He asserted that Knoll had followed him off Interstate 5 after having been accidentally cut off. Bowman alleged that Knoll became verbally enraged and heaved a bottle in his direction. Bowman feared for his life and retaliated by pulling out his loaded gun and firing.

His bad theatre played to an unreceptive audience. Knoll's death grip on the steering wheel, no evidence of an intact or shattered bottle and the sheer improbability of the tale did not impress the prosecution or jury.

The case proved uncomplicated. Yancy Knoll was simply beside Bowman's vehicle at the *wrong* moment when the perpetrator finally tested out his murder experiment.

Bowman was convicted of first-degree murder with a firearm enhancement and sentenced to 29 years and two months in prison. He is currently interned at the Clallam Bay Corrections Center.

Dinh Bowman was described throughout the trial as *detached* and *unremorseful*. At his hour-long sentencing hearing, he silently whimpered and wept throughout the proceedings. The enormity of his *thrill kill* and accompanying stupidity had finally sunk in. His mother Hong Bowman added irony to the hearing when she blamed herself for having encouraged her son to learn about guns for self-protection. She asked that she be allowed to serve her son's sentence for him.

When the pathetic Dinh Bowman spoke for himself amidst his tears, he could not beg for forgiveness from Knoll's family and friends. All that he could muster was *I'm disappointed that the jurors didn't believe me*.

The disconcerting case was aired on CBS's *48 Hours* television series numerous times. One of the primary fallouts from this exposure was the added degree of scrutiny shown towards Bowman's wife Jennifer. How much did she know about the killing and cover-up?

A practicing dentist at the time in Bainbridge Island, she avoided the trial, refused interviews, changed her last name and was captured on video exchanging baby babble with her husband under the moniker of *Bunny and Snuggles*. Police investigators questioned her regarding her role in cover-up attempts, but did not ultimately charge her as an accessory.

The general public has been less accommodating vilifying her online and tracking the relocation of her dental practice to Renton. She may never fully escape the taint of her husband's actions. Unlike Yancy Knoll, she is still living and able to work professionally.

Bad karma can be very punitive and unforgiving.

**Yancy Knoll's Murder Site:
Corner of 15th Avenue Northeast and Northeast 75th Street, Seattle**

James Elledge: A Rare Example of Legitimate Remorse?

James Elledge seemed to comprehend there persisted an inherent wickedness inside of him. The struggle between good and evil raged within his soul until ultimately the only conclusion he could arrive at was to allow society to put him to death.

The state of Washington obliged through his execution by lethal injection at the State Penitentiary in Walla Walla on August 28, 2001. The road to his ultimate demise raised many ethical issues based on whether an accused individual may opt to abandon any pretext of a defense argument and avoid appealing his conviction.

At his murder trial, Elledge made a full confession and refused to present a defense argument. Once condemned to a first-degree murder by a jury, he refused to allow the filing of any appeals against his sentence, much to the chagrin of anti-capital punishments advocacy groups.

James Elledge wanted to die as atonement for the evil that he perceived within himself. He got his wish.

His history was sordid. In 1965, Elledge robbed a Western Union office in Albuquerque, New Mexico and in the process kidnapped a female attendant. He was apprehended and spent time in a Santa Fe prison. Following his release, he migrated to Seattle. In 1974, he killed a motel manager Bertha Lush with a hammer during an argument over a bill. He served over twenty years for the crime and was paroled in August 1995.

Upon his release, his life began to resemble a miracle of forgiveness, acceptance and heartwarming reformation.

A member of a Lynnwood church befriended him upon his release from prison. The church fully embraced him into their membership and activities. They found him accommodations and employment as a janitor at the facility. His character overhaul proved illusionary.

For two years, the reformed Elledge accepted their warm kindness and hospitality. Betrayal and a return to his homicidal mania would resurface three years later. He felt that one of the church parishioners, Eloise Fitzner, 47, had attempted to sabotage his relationship with a woman that he ultimately married.

For a year, he plotted a means to seek his revenge. On April 18, 1998, Elledge invited the unsuspecting and naive Fitzner and a friend to a dinner in the basement Bible study room of the church. Upon their entrance into the room, he closed the door, pulled a knife and bound both women's wrists and ankles. He covered Fitzner's friend with a sweatshirt over her head and commanded her to face the wall away from her friend.

Elledge strangled Fitzner and then stabbed her fatally in the neck. He hid the body and then abducted her friend, who was terrified and powerless throughout the ordeal. He drove Fitzner's car to his house where he proceeded to sexually assault her. He then unexplainably released her the following day. She reported the killing to the police and he was arrested within two days.

While in prison, Elledge was credited with saving a guard's life during a riot and tipping off authorities to the escape plans of other inmates. In all likelihood, his execution would have been stayed through the normal appeal process,

A persistent theme in his published public and private statements stressed his conviction regarding his internal wickedness and the abnormally of his nature. His fate became a poignant examination over a prisoner's right to initiate voluntary euthanasia via the legal system.

The denial of an innate evil presence is common in the rationale of condemned individuals explaining their actions. Upbringing, mental illness, misfortune and even poverty become more convenient excuses. James Elledge was very clear about the condition of his soul. His resolution to unburden society of himself was a rare and curious example.

At his execution, he expressed deep remorse for killing Fitzner. One is inclined to believe his feelings were sincere. Sadly, his contrition could not ultimately spare the victims.

James Elledge Killing Site:
Lynnwood Free Methodist Church Basement, 6529 188th SW, Lynnwood

Jed Waits: Destroying the Infatuation He Could Not Possess

The infatuation began during their university studies at Seattle Pacific University. Jennifer Paulson and Jed Waits worked together in the school's cafeteria. They occasionally socialized with friends and co-workers outside of work as a group. A romantic chemistry never materialized in her mind. In Jed Waits imagination, she became everything.

They graduated and seemingly ventured off in differing directions. For six years while she was teaching in the Tacoma Unified School District, they had minimal contact. He would telephone annually, but his contact was unnerving. He often phoned ten to fifteen times in a single day. She would not respond immediately. Instead she would leave a voice message with her excuses several days later.

Waits would vanish until the each subsequent years call. In 2007, he was deployed into Kuwait with a National Guard Unit. His stint did not go well as he was disciplined repeatedly during his tenure. He was less than honorably discharged in April 2009.

In the spring of 2008, his obsession towards Paulson intensified. She was working at a Tacoma Elementary school as a special education teacher in the language resource center assisting students with reading problems. Waits would randomly show up at her school unannounced and once left flowers with a stuffed bear for her. Paulson had not informed him where she was working.

The school's principal called Waits' commander in the National Guard to inform him of the unwarranted attention. Paulson filed a restraining order against him in September

2008. Waits kept clear of her. He respected the terms until he assumed it expired one year later. Court records indicated that the harassment order remained valid until September 2010.

In February 2010, she noticed him following her as she was driving home from work. She telephoned 911 and the police dispatcher advised her to drive to a nearby police station. Waits was arrested that evening, but posted bail the following Monday. Paulson was justifiably terrified when she learned of his release. The menace was heading for a climatic conclusion.

Up to that point, Waits stalking appeared exclusively psychological. On Friday morning, February 26, 2010, his behavior turned lethal. He anticipated Paulson's arrival at her workplace and waited. By then, he was well acquainted with her daily routine, despite the fact she hadn't slept at her house out of fear the night before.

At 7:35 a.m. as she exited her car to approach the school, he advanced towards her along the concrete walkway leading to the main entrance. She was one of the first to arrive on the premises. It was not recorded if they exchanged any words. Waits was armed with a semi automatic weapon. His intention was decisive.

Paulson screamed to the extremity of her lungs, but to no avail. Waits callously shot her multiple times killing her instantly. Her body lay near the base of a large adjacent evergreen tree. He sprinted down the middle of the street fronting the school into his parked car.

He drove off in view of several eyewitnesses, His vehicle was tracked downed down soon afterwards approximately ten miles from the shooting scene. He was isolated in a parking lot of a daycare center. He engaged police officers in a brief shootout before turning the gun on himself and firing.

Jennifer Paulson understood the instability and desperate nature of Waits' obsession. Her terrifying premonition proved accurate. With the absence of any defined physical threat, she became vulnerable to a depressingly familiar scenario of someone destroying what they could not possess.

**Jennifer Ann Paulson Murder Site:
Birney Elementary School, 1202 S 76th Street, Tacoma**

Jeremy McLean: The Revenge Killing of A Drug Informant

Jeremy McLean understood the risks behind his consent. He possibly didn't realize the extent and length of time his commitment would require.

Jeremy, 26, was a small-scale Longview addict and drug dealer who had been arrested in 2006 on the charges of selling eight methadone pills to a Cowlitz-Wahkiakum County Narcotics Task Force member. Conviction of the charges potentially carried a three-year jail term. To avoid a trial, McLain opted to work as an undercover drug informant.

McLean signed an agreement with the regional law enforcement agency. The contract terminology acknowledged the risks and dangers involved and held the agencies harmless from liability.

One of the disturbing questions behind the agreement was whether McLean participation was volunteered or solicited by the drug task force. His own extended family had very significant ties to the region's law enforcement and legal communities. The answer was never clearly resolved.

One report indicated that McLean had approached the task force once his legal obligation had been fulfilled. He reportedly inquired as to the employment prospects for continued employment with compensation. His scenario and fate raised more questions than answers.

As the case with many part-time informants, McLean was untrained and inexperienced. Despite coaching efforts, it became unclear as to how much back up he was provided by law enforcement authorities.

During his brief tenure, he was credited with participating in twelve controlled buys, resulting in five arrests. Two such arrest involved heroin dealer William Vance Reagan, Jr. and his girlfriend, Victoria Gatti. Following two purchases in June and July 2008 by McLean while he was wired with a microphone, the pair were arrested the following month on drug charges.

Longview is a small town of 36,000. Rumors about McLean's activities began to compromise his confidential identity. Reagan was successfully able to identify McLean's by examining the disclosure documents in the case proceedings against him. He vowed that McLean would never take the witness stand to testify against him during his impending January 2009 trial.

McLean was forewarned of his dangerous predicament. The first evening Reagan was bailed out of jail, he telephoned McLean's mother himself and warned her of her son's impending fate. The threats were forwarded to law enforcement authorities, who discounted their source and severity.

McLean felt increasingly uneasy despite their assurances and reportedly slept within reach of a rifle awaiting an inevitable attack. His father indicated that he feared for his life and rarely left their house. During the time following his release on bail, Reagan was actively soliciting individuals to kill McLean. In the end, he completed the job himself.

It was documented in court records that detectives had warned McLean to keep a low profile and even offered to help him leave town. Where could he relocate? He refused the offer. Despite the heightened danger and awareness of risk, McLean was employed on one last fateful buy.

On December 29, 2008, an undetermined accomplice of Reagan lured McLean to a parked motor home for a drug purchase. Reagan was hiding in a bathroom armed with a .22 caliber pistol. McLean was cautious to the extent of paranoia upon entering the trailer. He carefully began checking behind a sealed closet door. At that instant, Reagan leapt out of a bathroom and shot him three times in the head.

As McLean expired in agony on the floor, Reagan finished him off in the face with a final round. McLean's body was pitched into the Colombia River. It was discovered beached on New Years Day by a fisherman on the banks of a county park site.

Investigators and family were certain from the beginning of the prime suspect. Reagan and Gatti were arrested four days later at a Portland, Oregon motel after a brief manhunt. Awaiting trial, Reagan had few effective escape options. He and Gatti surrendered without resistance.

He pleaded guilty to the killing in 2009 and was sentenced to life in prison without parole. He is currently interned in the Washington State Penitentiary in Walla Walla.

A lawsuit filed by McLean's family against the cities of Kelso and Longview and Cowlitz and Wahkiakum counties resulted in a $375.000 settlement. The law enforcement authorities conceded no liability accompanying their financial award.

The case briefly raised significant questions regarding the training and safety of informants and law enforcement's role in protecting them. Jeremy McLean became simply one more casualty in a ceaseless war on illegal drug distribution that shows absolutely no signs of receding.

**Jeremy McLean's Murder Site:
28th and Nichols, Longview**

Naveed Afzal Haq's Lone Rampage Against American Foreign Policy

Naveed Afzal Haq epitomized the lone wolf madness that extremist Islamic Jihadists have preached against western culture and civilization. The struggle is spiritual, inflexible and subject to grotesque misinterpretation. Haq found his target on Friday afternoon, July 28. 2006 when he stormed the Seattle Jewish Federation Building located in the Belltown district.

Haq, residing and simmering in distant Pasco, intended to strike a symbolic blow against the nation of Israel and its American representatives by engaging in a shooting rampage. His actions involved shooting six female employees, killing one.

Haq gained entry to the Federation's security protected building by holding an employee's 14-year-old niece hostage. Once inside the structure, Haq mounted a staircase to the second floor. He walked down the hallway, firing into offices with two semiautomatic handguns as he passed by. Three women were wounded in the abdomen area. Pamela Waechter was shot in the chest. As she attempted to flee down a flight of stairs, Haq callously reached over the railing and blasted her fatally a second time in the head.

In the course of his shooting spree, Haq threatened to kill anyone who attempted to telephone the police. He caught one of his wounded victims, five months pregnant and bleeding profusely speaking on the phone with a police dispatcher. He grabbed the telephone from her and announced that he was holding hostages.

He continued ranting and made demands to speak with the CNN news department. He stressed that he wanted to speak out against American foreign and military policy in the Middle East. The dispatcher calmly informed Haq that contacting CNN was impossible and ultimately would have no effect on U.S. policy.

Meditating briefly on the absurdity of his predicament, he informed the dispatcher he would surrender. He laid down his guns and walked silently out of the building with his hands on his head. The drama had lasted only fifteen minutes.

A SWAT team canvassed the building seeking other suspects and possible victims. Haq it was determined had no accomplices. He simply had a twisted agenda. Throughout the ordeal, he had repeatedly identified himself as a Muslim-American, but background research revealed that he had rarely visited a local mosque and had briefly even chosen to convert to Christianity. His actions proved an affront to both religions.

It was revealed following the carnage that Haq's two handguns had been purchased legally and had included a mandatory waiting period. He received the guns the day before his rampage. En route to the shooting, he had received a traffic ticket, but had done nothing to arouse the officer suspicions issuing the citation.

At his original April 2008 trial, the issue over seeking the death penalty dominated the early proceedings. Haq had a ten-year history of treatment for mental illness. Two of his shooting victims were also adamantly opposed to capital punishment. Initially, Haq surprised the court proceedings by indicating that he wanted to plead guilty to each of the nine counts of his indictment.

He changed his mind and plea six days later.

His first jury found him not guilty on one charge of attempted murder and could not reach consensus on the other eight counts. The judge declared the case a mistrial. His second trial was held late in 2009 and this time the jury found him guilty on all charges. He was sentenced to life without parole plus 120 years due to the *hate crime* status of the killings.

Haq is currently imprisoned at the Airway Heights Correction Center following a stint at the Washington State Penitentiary in Walla Walla, presumably in isolation. Although his intent and actions garnered no official support by any international Jihadist organization, Haq is hardly alone with his philosophical differences against American foreign policy.

Jihad is a declared war against the fundamental principals and morals behind western civilization. The rules of engagement in civilian war are very direct. There are neither innocent victims nor regulations to respect.

Jewish Federation Building Shooting Rampage: 2031 3rd Avenue, Seattle

The Dredged Trunk Recovery: Seattle's Mahoney Disappearance Scandal

Ex-convict Jim Mahoney, 36, arrived into Seattle in 1920 after serving only two years of a longer prison sentence. He had been a railroad worker from Milwaukee and was convicted of drugging and robbing a man in Spokane.

His abbreviated 5-8 year sentence resulted from his mother's connections with then Washington Governor, Louis Hart. Mahoney joined his family and sought more lucrative prospects in Seattle.

He found his ideal opportunity in 68-year-old Kate Mooers, whose recent divorce from a doctor left her rich and lonely. She was no beauty but maintained an enviable real estate portfolio coupled by an extreme penchant for thrift.

It became an instant infatuation when they were introduced…at least for her. The seduction was brief and a marriage quickly following in February 1921. The Mahoneys began making plans for an extensive honeymoon scheduled to begin in mid-April.

Kate Mooers-Mahoney withdrew money from her bank on Friday, April 15. She informed neighbors and friends that the ecstatic couple would be departing the following evening on a month-long train visit to the East Coast. No one saw the couple off at the train station.

Jim Mahoney returned to Seattle eleven days later alone. He explained that his bride had remained back East and was scheduling an excursion to Cuba with her friends.

For the next two weeks, he managed her properties and forged power-of-attorney documents to gain access to her assets. He lived extravagantly and quickly raised the suspicions of her friends and relatives. He offered a bevy of excuses to explain her delay in returning.

Two of Kate's nieces contacted Seattle police detectives. Mahoney suddenly turned silent. The nieces presented investigators with comparative samples of her handwriting to demonstrate Mahoney's intentions based on financial requests. The different signatures eliminated any sense of legitimacy attached to letters arriving to her friends and family reassuring them of her safety.

Further police investigation revealed that Mahoney had hired a moving company on the evening of April 16 to transfer a heavy steamer trunk from one of the Mahoney's buildings. Further, he had chartered a boat to transfer the trunk to a houseboat he reportedly had inquired about renting but never did.

The last view of the trunk was with him aboard the boat paddling out into the darkness and frigid waters of Lake Union. He never returned the boat, but it was retrieved approximately a week later sunk in shallow water.

His constructed plan of deceit began unraveling as additional witnesses testified to further questionable activities including a woman posing as Kate Mahoney. His trail of duplicity (and stupidity) tied him to a purchase of 30 feet of hemp rope and 5 pounds of quicklime. Predictably he had the audacity to charge the purchases to Kate's store account.

Everything about Jim Mahoney pointed to her disappearance and his guilt. The police anticipated his flight. They had placed him under surveillance for three weeks. As he prepared his escape, he was arrested despite the protestations of his lawyers. When he was detained, he had $25,000 worth of Kate's jewelry stuffed in his pockets.

Investigators suspected that he had dumped the steamer trunk near the northeastern end of Lake Union. Their instincts proved correct. They dredged the Portage Bay sector and divers found it near the bottom anchored to a large chunk of cement by hemp rope.

The face of the corpse inside had been eaten away by the quicklime, but the body was still identifiable as Kate Mooers-Mahoney. Her autopsy ruled that she'd been given a lethal dose of morphine and jammed into the trunk while still alive. Blows from a heavy object had crushed her skull.

Jim Mahoney's trial followed in September. The prosecution laid out a clear pattern of his scheming, deceit and motive reinforced by numerous witnesses. The defense had their own witness claiming the body found was not Mrs. Mahoney and that she had been seen after April 16th.

The jury discounted their testimony and found him guilty of first-degree murder. He appealed the conviction over the next eleven months without success. He was hung at the State Penitentiary in Walla Walla on December 1, 1922.

It seems difficult to conceive the expediency of justice from that era. Within a span of less than two years, Jim Mahoney had been released from prison, married a wealthy widow, killed her for her assets, underwent trial, appealed unsuccessfully and then was executed.

Proponents of the death penalty stress the importance of quick implementation once a judgment is rendered. Swift justice establishes the death sentence as a detrimental factor in discouraging crime. The current snail pace of execution and lengthy appeals process render the fear factor amongst criminals negligible.

Opponents cite the existence of numerous cases where poorly represented defendants have been executed unjustly. Many still maintain that capital punishment is unconstitutional and is merely cruel and unusual punishment. Their argument is irrespective of the circumstances behind the killer's victim(s) death.

The question and answer remains divided and is raised repeatedly for judicial debate and interpretation. Is society better served by the excessive delay for condemned individuals?

**Mahoney Residence Site:
409 Denny Way, Seattle**

Pang Frozen Food Fire: An Empire of Achievement Devoured In An Evening's Flames

Mary Pang built an impressive empire of frozen Chinese food products from her sister's original concept.

Her sister was Ruby Chow, who made her own reputation as a famed Seattle restaurateur and King County councilwoman. Chow was also known for having employed actor Bruce Lee at her restaurant during his Seattle student years.

Pang's operation was the epitome of energetic entrepreneurship. Her operations were hands-on, cost efficient and a model for any enterprise to emulate. She was raised in South Seattle to immigrant Chinese parents and attended Franklin High School. Even more impressively, she studied at the University of Washington, a feat for any woman of her era.

Everything about Mary Pang radiated prosperity and good fortune. Her distinctive red and yellow boxes of egg rolls lined freezer sections of supermarkets nationally. Her business was an inseparable extension of herself and family. She gave generously to the community. She passed on her knowledge of Chinese cooking through a published cookbook and instruction to thousands of students.

In the early 1960s, her family enterprise purchased an older warehouse facility on the outskirts of Seattle's International District to operate their expanding empire. The building had eluded extensive safety inspections for many years before a fateful January evening.

At 7:00 p.m. on January 5, 1995, a member of a band who practiced in the facility reported a fire to police. A group of

Seattle firefighters raced into the burning warehouse to extinguish the flames unaware that the building had a basement. The fragile structure soon became an inferno and the floor collapsed. Four firefighters, Lt. Walter Kilgore, Lt. Gregory Shoemaker, Randall Terlicker and James Brown plunged to their death into a still burning basement below. Seven other firefighters inside barely escaped the collapse.

The age and condition of the building created an untenable situation. The flames raged unabated for hours despite the efforts of multiple fire crews. Rescue efforts for the missing firefighters became impossible.

Three days later, the bodies of the fallen firefighters were recovered. The Seattle Fire Department was heavily criticized for their hasty response without prior knowledge of the building's structural composition. Previous arson threats to the building had not been recorded for the benefit of the responding firemen.

Conspicuously missing in the aftermath of the fire was Mary Pang's adopted son Martin. Unlike his mother, Martin enjoyed a lifestyle of extravagance without the burden of tireless work. He fled to Brazil. As investigator's sifted laboriously through the wreckage, their conclusion of arson was confirmed.

Martin Pang remained the sole suspect. His motive for torching the structure was his desire to collect the resulting insurance proceeds. He selected his escape destination judiciously. He was extradited back to the United States in 1996 to face lesser manslaughter charges instead of murder. Brazil agreed to the transfer only under those conditions since they had no arson felony murder statute equivalent to Washington's.

He pled guilty to four counts of manslaughter and was sentenced to a 35-year term. As part of his sentencing and due to subsequent civil lawsuits, he was ordered to pay restitution to the victim's families totaling approximately $5.4 million.

His actions while incarcerated have indicated an absolute lack of contrition, despite denials by his attorney. In 2013 he was alleged to have contacted a co-conspirator on the outside to initiate an elaborate identity theft ring. The scam targeted the firefighters, officers and witnesses involved in his case. His motive appeared to be revenge.

The scheme was discovered and never materialized. He was not formally charged for the attempt, but lost the reduced time he'd earned on his sentence for good behavior.

The fire and accompanying fatalities forced the Seattle Fire Department to re-evaluated operational procedures, tighten building inspections and more accurately archive building structural design information. The slain firefighters are commemorated by four bronze sculptures lodged in Pioneer Square.

The Mary Pang frozen food business closed permanently following the blaze. The family name would become synonymous with the tragedy. Her husband's health declined shortly afterwards and she shifted her attentions from the business towards his care. He died in 2004. Her renowned sister Ruby Chow would precede her in death by one year. In March 2009, Mary Pang passed away from a heart attack at the age of 87.

Her years of struggle and persistence dissipated with the arson fire. What becomes the worst irony to that decline is that her imprisoned son, being the sole heir, inherited the entire family estate upon his release.

In 2015, acting as his own legal council, Martin Pang attempted to dodge his impending financial obligations to the victim's families by challenging the terminology of the payback terms. A three-judge Court of Appeals ruled unanimously against his petition.

On September 27, 2018, Martin Pang was released from the State Prison in Walla Walla after having served 23 years. He arranged his own ride and was released with $40 of gate money, two boxes of possessions, and a guitar. Pang still owed $3.2 million in restitution to the families of the fallen firefighters with the payment due to begin a month after his prison release. A follow-up announcement as to whether he's made those payments has remained unpublished. A no contact order was also in place preventing Pang from having any contact with the families. It was reported in newspapers that he has moved to Prosser.

The sin of the unworthy son has forever tainted the family legacy. Equally clear is the fate and lesson offered towards those who plead their own legal cases. His outcome was as appropriate as predictable.

**Pang Food Fire Site:
811 Seventh Avenue at Dearborn, Seattle**

Patrick Drum: A Self-Appointed One Man Hit Squad Against Sexual Predators

At the age of 34, Patrick Drum determined the focus for his remaining life. The Olympic Peninsula resident decided that he would lead a one-man vigilante crusade against convicted sex offenders.

This individual judge, jury and executioner preached publicly at his murder trial that his actions were intended *to protect the community's children*. Agreement with his motives was far from consensual within the communities of Sequim and adjacent Port Angeles, where he'd resided most of his life.

On the evening of June 2, 2012, Drum shot 28-year-old Gary Blanton, Jr. multiple times within a confined Sequim residential cottage they shared. The killing was muddled and clumsy. Blanton had time to call police while he was being wounded in the pitch darkness. He finally succumbed to his injuries while on the telephone.

The following sunrise, Drum drove to the outskirts of Port Angeles where he pounded on the residential front door of 57-year-old Jerry Ray. A surprise assault was imperative to his plans. No one answered. He came back after steadying his nerves via a brief walk around the neighborhood.

When he returned, Drum simply burst through front door and surprised a disoriented Ray responding to the noise from his bedroom. He shot the backpedaling Ray three times killing him. He had erroneously anticipated Ray to be armed.

The two victims were part of a larger agenda of 60 names that Drum had compiled. Each listing was a registered sex offender living in Peninsula towns including Forks, Sequim, Port Angeles and Quilcene. Drum had isolated individuals who had been charged with rape or other serious crimes.

His ambitious project would require time. He had prepared a backpack stuffed with camouflage clothing, topographical maps, a bag full of cannabis and supplies for living in the wilderness. His intention was to blend into the landscape during the agreeable summer months as a survivalist. He planned to emerge periodically to eliminate additional targeted victims.

In the cases of Blanton and Ray, his motives were personal. With Blanton, questions remained as to how warranted was his target.

In 2000, Drum had become friends with Blanton's future wife during periods of their drug addiction and rehab sessions together. She would later meet and marry Blanton who had his own reckless and violent history. By her account, his life stabilized after marriage and the birth of their two children.

When he was 17, Blanton pled guilty to violating a 17-year-old deaf/mute girl. His wife and mother argued that the sex had been consensual since they'd been dating and the girl set him up. Since both were minors, his actions constituted statutory rape.

Blanton's background concerned Drum. What he found most intolerable about the couple's relationship were two unusual injuries one of their children suffered. Their 17-month old son sustained a traumatic spiral fracture that would have required great force to provoke. A primary example would be a young child being forcefully grabbed by their arm by an angry parent. A second two-week-old fracture on the same child's thighbone appeared even more suspicious. The fracture convinced an attending doctor that the child had become the victim of child abuse at the hands of the father.

Blanton was arrested and released on bail with the condition that he stay away from his children. Drum had maintained his distance from the couple but decided upon a solution.

During Blanton's separation from his family, Drum paid a visit to him at his temporary lodgings. An observation of Blanton's careless and negligent attitude towards his host convinced him his project was just. During one visit, he engaged the lodger in a fistfight. Once their passions cooled, he did something completely out of character. He invited Blanton to reside with him in his small cottage.

Blanton readily accepted having few options. For a brief time, Drum masqueraded as a concerned friend. The guise fooled both Blantons. Drum however merely wanted his prey in close proximity when he launched his eventual plan.

Jerry Ray was an even more loathsome target in Drum's eyes. Drum claimed that he personally knew two of his molestation victims. He had been acquainted with the pair since their youth and often took them fishing when they were teenagers.

Ray had pleaded guilty in 2002 to raping a 7-year old and 4-year old, which he blamed on inebriation. He served no jail time and was under state supervision classified as a moderate-risk-level offender. He was then living as a caregiver for his aged father suffering from numerous ailments. His father would discover his son's body shortly after the shooting as he emerged from his adjacent bedroom.

With both victims, Drum left a note cryptically justifying his actions and a signature lollipop. After killing Ray, he abandoned his rental car in the woods and hitched a ride with a trucker heading towards Quilcene to resume his killing spree. He wrongly assumed that he had a solid head start. He was unaware that Ray's father had already telephoned police and roadblocks were being simultaneously constructed.

Viewing the barricades from a distance, Drum exited the truck and headed for a forest on foot. The trucker tipped off police and following a three-hour manhunt, he was apprehended,

Drum's own tainted background was littered by a criminal past. He had been convicted for residential burglary, tampering with a witness, drug possession, possession of stolen property and unlawful issuance of checks. Part of his own revenge motivation might have originated from his father's history and pattern of sexual abuse with young women. His father had a conviction for statutory rape.

Most of his family and friends stressed that he was in the process of rehabilitating his life. He was unemployed at the time of the killings.

He attributed his fresh calling to a mentor and friendship that he had cultivated while in prison. His focus of protecting the innocent enabled him to experience a sense of accomplishment and social importance. In his eyes, these objectives were the keys towards personal redemption.

The legal system, however, simply identified his actions as calculated murder.

At his trial, he spoke with a swagger admitting no remorse for killing the two men. He minimized their surviving families and friends as *unfortunate collateral damage*. His message was not universally well received by many in attendance. He had, however, cultivated his own local supporter base. The trial was contentious with derogatory name calling traded between sides. The venomous scorn had minimal effect on the self-professed avenging martyr.

He was convicted by a jury of first-degree murder and sentenced to life imprisonment without the possibility of parole.

Jail proved a scant deterrent to his ambitions. During his first week of incarceration, he stabbed a 19-year-old sex offender inmate. The prisoner would recover and Drum was transferred into solitary confinement. He was reported to have attempted another killing months later following his release from isolation. He is currently imprisoned at the Washington Corrections Center in Shelton following a stint at the Clallam Bay Corrections Center.

His pattern and ambitions are clear. He is not alone with his intentions. It is widely known that within prison circles, inmates consistently target sexual predators. Amongst the earliest identification signs are sharp cuts administered to a sexual offender's extremities effectively labeling them. The markings are not life threatening, but alerts to the general prison population. Subsequent violent attacks will follow.

A direct tracing between an inmate's formation and ultimate incarceration is usually accompanied by severe patterns of childhood neglect and abuse. Within many prison populations, a mentality exists that inmates have the easiest access and capability of eradicating the problem at its source.

Clinical and published medical treatments attempting to cure pedophilia and molestation have proven statistically ineffective. As an extreme measure, many child protection proponents advocate life imprisonment or death for carriers of such an incurable disease. Rehabilitation in their eyes remains impossible. They argue that the risk inherent to future innocent victims is too profound. As evidenced through Patrick Drum's eyes, he was merely cleaning out *society's trash*.

A critical question remains. Should someone with his background and obsession have such a right? Society and the legal system currently say no.

Gary Blanton, Jr. Murder Site: 5011 Sequim-Dungeness Way, Sequim

Jerry Ray's Murder Site: 31 Heuhslein Road, Port Angeles

Peter Keller: The Survivalist Killer Who Ultimately Couldn't Hide

In the demented mind of 41 year-old Peter Keller, he had fabricated an untraceable escape location. He envisioned an extended fugitive life once he had slain his wife Lynnettee, also 41, and daughter Kaylene, 19.

No one was able to answer precisely why he wanted to kill them.

Keller had constructed an elaborate bunker inside an elevated incline on isolated Rattlesnake Ridge located within ten miles of the North Bend condominium that he shared with his wife and daughter. His plan following their murder was to vanish into the terrain and exist as a survivalist. His ambitions included building laboratories for viruses and nanobots.

His bunker, which he called *Camp Keller*, became an obsession that consumed eight years of his leisure hours and weekends. He informed his wife and daughter that the impending end of the world necessitated the project. He never revealed the location to them and they didn't appear concerned.

Lynnettee was disabled, remaining principally at home and concentrated on crafts and scrapbooking projects, which she sold online and at fairs. Kaylene was a Bellevue community college student with a steady boyfriend who regularly visited their house. Family and friends expressed surprise by Keller's actions noting a loving relationship with his daughter.

Keller resolutely controlled the family finances and excluded them from access. His wife's only consistent income was from a state disability payment she received after a workplace accident several years before. She was often obliged to borrow money from family members.

Peter Keller concealed their income through several bank accounts. By the time he was ready to initiate his plan, he had stored tens of thousands of dollars bundled in his bunker.

He extensively documented his design, which featured PVC pipes running into the bunker that diverted water from a nearby stream. A rope and pulley system was used to pull substantial logs into place. His bunker was encased within a cement foundational core and featured a wood-burning stove. He operated a generator to provide power inside.

Keller had stocked an arsenal with stacks of ammunition, explosive devices, several high-powered rifles and body armor. He was prepared for a siege that he hoped he might evade through extensive camouflage. His plan appeared solid. Theoretically, he should have eluded capture indefinitely.

On April 22, 2012, firefighters responded to a blaze inside the Keller's elevated home. Arson was obvious with the discovery of seven gas cans inside on the floor and the front door barricaded by furniture. Lynnettee and Kaylene were found dead in their beds with bullet wounds to their head. Neither had anticipated their attack based on earlier phone conversations hours before their deaths.

The fire was intended to destroy all evidence of his site planning and location. He had kept dozens of revealing digital photographs in an open safe that were meant to be consumed. The blaze was contained before the photos were destroyed. The images enabled investigators to pinpoint the bunker's location by showing distinctive power lines and the North Bend outlet mall. Keller's remaining electronics devices, computer, cell phone records and sightings of his red pickup truck identified the Rattlesnake Ridge location within five days.

One may conceal themselves, but disappearance becomes nearly impossible with contemporary surveillance equipment. Peter Keller thought he had built the perfect hideout. He had simply constructed his own mausoleum. As SWAT teams began to encircle his escape access, they observed footprints from his military style boots, the smell of smoke from his woodstove and lights flickering on and off inside his bunker.

The police began their assault by firing tear gas inside with no effect. The canisters were either not introduced deep enough or Keller was prepared with a gas mask. He had anticipated such a climatic confrontation for eight years. Now less than a week after launching his grandiose vision, he was surrounded and doomed.

Keller responded by firing a single pistol shot into his mouth. He died instantly, but his body wasn't recovered until the following day for fear of rigged booby traps. Left behind was a videotape describing in sobering and rambling details the rationale behind his actions. He claimed to be okay with death should his ambitions fail. He shed no understanding as to why his wife and daughter were obliged to share his fate.

Peter Keller's descent into obsession and madness offered no insight into why he sensed the world was approaching its culmination. Instead, it portrayed a paranoid loner's justification for exiting a world he felt permanently estranged from.

**Peter Keller's Family Killing Site:
1525 Rock Creek Ridge SW, North Bend**

Rattlesnake Ridge

Rafay Family Murders: The Damning Conversations That Sabotaged A Perfect Alibi

Atif Rafay and Sebastian Burns constructed the perfect alibi for their activities on the evening of July 12, 1994. The pair ate dinner at a Bellevue Factoria neighborhood restaurant and viewed a late night showing of *The Lion King* in the same shopping center afterwards. Afterwards, they crossed the Interstate 90 Bridge to Seattle and attempted to attend a Belltown district nightclub near the monorail stop. They were turned away because the club was soon closing.

At each location, numerous witnesses confirmed their presence. No one was able to confirm that they had sat through the entire showing of the film.

At approximately 2 a.m., they returned to Rafay's home to discover his parents and sister had been slain. They telephoned police.

The killings were committed during the screening of the film. Rafay's parent's Tariq and Sultana and his developmentally disabled sister, Basma, were beaten to death with an aluminum baseball bat in their affluent Sommerset district residence in Bellevue. The duo-level house and lot are sizable and none of their neighbors reported any unusual entrances or sounds throughout the evening.

Sultana was bludgeoned to death from behind while unpacking boxes in their basement. Tariq was beaten while lying in bed. The cruelest murder was committed to Basma, who vainly attempted to resist her attackers. She was found barely moaning when police arrived and died a few hours after her parents.

The vicious murders were motivated by one of the oldest of family motivations, inheritance money.

The Rafay family had lived in Vancouver for many years and was integrated deeply into the city's Muslim community. Tarif held a doctorate in engineering and had moved the family to Bellevue in 1993 to work at Alpha Engineering. Sultana had a masters degree in nutrition and devoted the majority of her time to caring for their 20-year-old daughter who hadn't spoken a discernible word for fifteen years.

Rafay and Burns made the crime scene appear to be a botched burglary. The house was in disarray, but nothing of value was missing. Police immediately suspected the pair but lacked solid evidence and nothing to refute the appearance of an airtight alibi.

Both men were eighteen at the time of the killing. Atif had just completed his freshman year at Cornell University. He had been visiting Burns at his West Vancouver home before both took a bus to visit his family.

The attack came only a week after their arrival. Three days afterwards, having been publicly dismissed by police as suspects, both returned to Canada. They began spending the family inheritance, which was estimated at a half million American dollars.

The Bellevue Police department officially named the pair as suspects six months later. Both confidently felt they were distant from the Bellevue police department's reach with their residence across the border. During early 1995, the Royal Canadian Mounted Police began their own investigation into the murders and subsequent fraud.

The department launched an elaborate five-month sting operation having officers pose as high stakes gambling mobsters. The intention of the program was to obtain DNA samples and gain confessions by bugging Atif and Burn's residence, telephone and car. As bait for seducing their involvement, the pair was promised a production role in an upcoming film. The gambit played on their greed and arrogance and worked to perfection.

The Canadian police recorded over four thousand hours of audio conversations, including conclusive confessions of the murders. Shortly a year after the killings, police would arrest both. Six years after subsequent legal wrangling, vehement protests by the suspects over their rights violations and extradition imposed conditions, Rafay and Burns were put on trial in the United States.

One of the quirkiest incidents accompanying the various delays was Burns being caught with his pants down by two guards outside of a King County Jail conference room. Shielding him and his erect penis from exposure was his flamboyant female defense attorney. Her own long dress was pulled up around her waist. Her unconventional defense posture, which she publicly downplayed as a *hug gone bad* forced her removal as counsel. She was suspended from the Washington Bar for two years.

The chilling confessional tapes effectively condemned the murderers. In particular, Burn's casual description of Basma's resistance prompted laughter from both men on tape. The account nauseated the jury. Burns physically committed the savage beatings when Atif lost his nerve. Instead, he coldly observed his family being decimated before his eyes. He yanked out a VCR in a futile effort to make the entry resemble a break-in. His amateur attempt fooled no one.

Without the taped confessions however, the prosecution's case against both men would have been nearly impossible to prove. Both were convicted of first-degree murder and sentenced to three consecutive life sentences. A condition of their Canadian extradition was that the death penalty could not be imposed.

Both men argued vehemently against the conviction and methods employed of evidence accumulation at their sentencing hearing. Both stressed that their confessions were coerced. Both maintained they were elsewhere when the killings were committed. Neither expressed remorse to acknowledge their wrong. Until the end, they were certain the act was ideally planned and executed.

The jury discarded their words. They concluded the evidence proving their guilt was overwhelming.

Glen Sebastian Burns and Atif Rafay are currently imprisoned at the same Monroe Correctional Complex, a rare occurrence for two individuals condemned for the same crime. They have the rest of their lives to determine why their perfect alibi fizzled. With the rampant existence of jailhouse snitches housed in legal correctional facilities, it would be probable to assume they've since learned silence and discretion in their personal communications with each other.

**Rafay Family Murders:
4610 144th Place SE, Bellevue**

The Detonation of Samuel Lau's Demons

The person Samuel Lau detonated similarly as the fireworks he sold on Monday morning, June 16, 1997. He shot his wife Arlene, 49 and his two sons Sammy, 21 and Terence, 17 several times in the upper body in the upstairs bedroom of his multi-leveled Bellevue home.

He composed a lengthy note of several pages blaming *business and personal reasons* for his actions. The text rambled on about accepting responsibility for the shootings and seeking forgiveness, but did not provide a specific motive.

Samuel Lau, then raised the same 9-mm pistol and shot himself to death in the head leaving an enigma without a solution.

He had operated a third-generation family fireworks business. By all accounts, he managed the operation successfully. He had evolved his role in the business to predominately becoming a broker. He sold principally to states that condoned firework sales including Washington, Missouri, Ohio and Texas.

He regularly expressed pride in his son's academic accomplishments. All of his newspaper quoted family and acquaintances indicated he was popular, effervescent and content. He had expressed worries before the shooting about competitive pressures mounting with his business, but detailed none of these to anyone.

The major pre-warning sign preceding his rampage was that he had begun taking tranquilizers a few months earlier. He had recently sold the family's Amherst neighborhood house and was planning a move to a larger residence. He traveled regularly to Hong Kong and had just returned the week before the killings.

In even the most tranquil and seemingly well-adjusted families, fissures may exist below the superficial surface. The private turmoil in Lau's mind that prompted such a desperate act was never publicly revealed. He suppressed his inner demons until he could no longer fend off the spirits that ultimately consumed him.

No one can still answer why.

**Samuel Lau Family Murder-Suicide:
13820 SE 62nd Street, South Bellevue**

An Asian Gangland Slaying During A Turbulent Tacoma Era

During the early morning of July 5, 1998 at 1:30 a.m., three masked members of a Tacoma gang entered the Trang Dai Café and opened fire on patrons in the karaoke bar. Two other gunmen from the gang kept watch in the back of the building.

Four men were killed including Nahn Ai Nguyen, Duy Le, Hai Le and Tuong Hung. A fifth fatality, waitress Tuyen Vo, was added as she attempted to flee the building. Five others were wounded including the primary target of the attack.

The killers fled. Within two weeks Tacoma police conducted an expansive search of nine homes seeking eight suspects. During the initial raid, they arrested five including Jimmie Chea, Marvin Leo, Veasna Sok, Sarun Truck Ngeth and John Phet.

As police hemmed in the suspected organizer, 22 year-old Ri Le, killed his younger half-brother, 17-year old Khanh Trinh and them himself as part of a murder-suicide pact. A seventh suspect, Le Tuan Anh was later arrested and an eighth, Samath Mom, committed suicide in jail shortly after his detainment.

Tacoma suffered an extremely adverse reputation during the latter decades of the Millennium due to an active youth gang presence, crime and violence. Their police department made eradicating the gang presence a priority in a focused attempt to reclaim territory and encourage future investment and growth. The community has rebounded significantly from that era when the downtown resembled a vacant war zone.

The Trang Dai massacre was a major wake-up call to arms.

The neighborhood of the crime site today appears tranquil and far removed from graffiti and evident organized gang activity. Appearances are not always absolute within a culture closed to outsiders.

The eight gang members that were accountable for the massacre were primarily teenagers at the time of the shooting. Their lives, like those of their victims, were irreparably altered by a violent reaction to an insignificant grudge. Tacoma police effectively dismantled the Loc'd Out Crips gang with their arrests.

Each of the detained were convicted and sentenced to prison terms based on the severity of their respective roles. Jimmee Chea and remains currently interned at the Washington State Penitentiary in Walla Walla. Marvin Leo and John Phet are imprisoned at the Washington Corrections Center in Shelton. Veasna Sok, Sarun Truck Ngeth and Le Tuan Anh are no longer listed on the state prison rolls and presumably have served out their terms.

A sad and destructive chapter of Tacoma history passed. The community continues its movement forward to fully regain back their streets.

**Trang Dail Karaoke Bar Massacre:
3819 S. Yakima, Tacoma**

Wah Mee Gambling Club: A Massacre That Shook The Foundations of An Illegal Seattle Tradition

Seattle's Pioneer Square and the adjacent International District are the center of a bawdy era of Seattle's historical past. The current Pioneer Square district was constructed as a second layer atop the foundations of the original city.

The International District was called Chinatown for decades due to the highly concentrated Asian population and ethnically related restaurants and shops. Secret fraternal societies called Tongs still occupy some of the prominent district buildings. Illicit high-stakes gambling traditionally flourished among some of the indistinct clandestine spaces.

These illegal activities were exposed to an unaware public on February 19, 1983, when fourteen gamblers were executed in the basement of the intimate Wah Mee Club located in Maynard Alley. Thirteen victims were bound and shot in the head at close range to eliminate any witnesses.

For the perpetrators, Kwan Fai *Willie* Mak, Wai-Chiu *Tony* Ng and Benjamin Ng, an unlikely fourteenth potential victim survived and escaped. He was able to testify against the three during their highly publicized trial. The thirteen deaths made the massacre the worst in Washington's history. The primary motive for the massacre was robbery. Mak had lost heavily at the club and wanted to recoup his losses.

The covert location featured a security system of passing through several successive doors ensuring absolute secrecy and discretion. The killers were members of the club enabling them direct accessibility. Several of the patrons killed were renowned and highly regarded within the

Chinese community. Publication of their names is noticeably absent in most public accounts, with the exception of the lone survivor.

During February 1983, Benjamin Ng and Willie Mak were charged with thirteen counts of aggravated first-degree murder. Tony Ng was charged in absentia having fled to Canada. The defendants hired a well-known Seattle legal team but to little avail. Benjamin Ng was convicted of murder and sentenced to life in prison. He is current interned at the Washington State Penitentiary in Walla Walla. Willie Mak was convicted of murder and sentenced to death. Following several appeals and stays of executions, he remains at the Monroe Correctional Complex.

Tony Ng was apprehended in Canada and tried in 1985. He was convicted on 13 counts of first-degree armed robbery and second-degree assault. He was exonerated on first-degree murder charges. He was sentenced to 35 years in prison. In 2013, to the astonishment of the victim's families, friends and public, he was paroled and deported to Hong Kong.

The basement club was shuttered immediately after the murders and frozen in time. On Christmas Eve, 2013, a fire gutted the top floor of the nearly vacant building. The damaged portion of the structure was demolished in April 2015.

Today, illicit gambling dens have become essentially replaced with the proliferation of legalized wagering and casinos on Native American lands. Fortunes are still made, but more commonly lost through an addiction that transcends time and culture.

**Wah Mee Gambling Club Massacre:
665 South King Street, (Maynard Alley) Seattle**

A Murder-Suicide Leaving A Perpetrator in Purgatory

On the early morning following another unhappy Christmas, Kevin Heimsoth decided to terminate the life of all of the immediate cohabitators in his residence. With his front door firmly secured preventing escape, he loaded a five-cartridge .38 caliber revolver and shot his 58-year-old wife Lynn in the head while she slept. Over the course of the evening, he would load the gun three times and kill both Lynn's comfort dog *Sukha* and the family cat.

He then accessed his Twitter account online and typed *Guns don't kill people, people do. AR-15s makes it super easy. I jsit (sic) killed my whole family, and I couldnt have done it without a gun!*

He would continue his rant on additional subjects solely expressing remorse for having killed Sukha. He sent four tweets in total shortly after 3 a.m. Satisfied that he had completed his mission, he sat on a couch with his revolver, pointed it to his head and pulled the trigger.

All had gone according to his plans *except* that he survived the wound. He was taken to a nearby hospital and then later airlifted to Harborview Hospital in Seattle. He remained in the Intensive Care Unit monitored by deputies at his bedside.

Neighbors would enter the house at 10 a.m. via a spare key after Lynn had not responded to their urgent texts. They were concerned after hearing cracking noises hours before.

Kevin Heimsoth had purchased the murder weapon from a local pawnshop. Deputies would find at least five bullet impact holes in the drywall and closet door where he was discovered. These may have been missed shots as he attempted to kill the pets. Lynn Heimsoth was fervently anti-firearms. She had been a paraeducator at Marysville Pilchuck High School during the October 2014 shooting when five students were shot to death. At the time of her murder, she was the Principal at Sunnyland Elementary School in Bellingham.

On January 1, 2020, a sheriff's deputy interviewed Kevin Heimsoth in his hospital room. The perpetrator was able to respond to yes or no questions through the use of his thumb. Having had a week to review his actions and probable future, Heimsoth expressed a very different version of events from his posted twitter messages. He claimed that he was not responsible for the shootings but knew who the killer was. He promised to reveal the guilty party when he would be physically able to do so.

Charges against Heimsoth were ultimately dismissed due to his wounds in November 2020. He became severely mentally disabled and a judge determined that he was unable to stand trial. Perhaps the most vicious punishment for him will be to continue to remain in physical and mental purgatory aware that he neither got away with murder nor removed himself fully from facing responsibility.

**Heimsoth Murder Residence:
909 Marine Drive #120, Bellingham**

Sex Offender Slaying Defines A Lone Vigilante Crusade

On July 13, 2005, Michael Anthony Mullen, 36 declared a vigilante crusade against sex offenders. He attributed his decision to his own past abuse and the Idaho child abduction and murder case of Joseph Edward Duncan that saturated the headlines that year.

His essential strategy began when he accessed the Whatcom County Sheriff's sex offender website and selected at least two potential victims. The site included their residential addresses as they were obliged to register with local authorities. One selected was currently under supervision by the Department of Corrections and the other released from supervision two years previously.

He visited three sex offenders, including the pair, sharing a Bellingham residence at approximately 9 p.m. of August 27th. He dressed in a blue jumpsuit and wore an FBI cap. Over beers, he identified himself as an agent wishing to discuss their legal status. For at least two hours, he informed them that they were on an Internet *hit site*. One of the men left the conversation to go to his workplace. He would return four hours later to find both of his roommates dead from gunshot wounds. Mullen indicated that he allowed the third party to leave because he had expressed remorse for his actions, but also added that he wanted a witness to understand his motive for the killings.

Slain were Victor Vasquez, 68 and Hank Eisses, 49, each killed by a single shot to the head. Vasquez was convicted in 1991 of molesting several relatives, each enduring habitual physical and sexual abuse. Eisses was sentenced to over five years in prison during 1997 for raping a 13-year-old boy at his home in Sumas, Washington. Both were classified as Level III sex offenders, considered individuals most likely to reoffend. Eisses was the owner of the house.

During the week and a half following the murders, Mullen mailed letters explaining the killings to several news outlets. The letters threatened the lives of future sexual predators, Before he could carry out his threat, family members encouraged him to telephoned police to turn himself in. His own past included a history of petty crime in Washington and California. He had no fixed address in Bellingham.

During his 2006 trial, he was convicted of first-degree murder and sentenced to a 44-year prison term. Some viewed his actions as heroics, but during his incarceration he was moved frequently from prison to prison. At the beginning of 2006, he wrote a letter to the *Seattle Times* stating: *facts are, I just want to die*.

On April 15, 2007, he was found unresponsive in his jail cell at Stafford Creek Corrections Center near Aberdeen. His death was classified a suicide. Five years later, his killings would spur Patrick Drum from Sequim to replicate his actions with the murder of two registered sex offenders. Drum knew the victims of the two men he killed.

There is little issue that the vicious cycle of sexual abuse to children often results in the victims becoming abusers as well. Mullen and Drum's solitary crusades became retaliatory protests against an evil that bears tarnished fruit. Yet the question persists, did they have the right to act as judge, jury and executioner?

**Residential Murder Site:
2825 Northwest Avenue, Bellingham**

Maurice Clemmons: A Lifetime of Debauchery Ends in Unnecessary Sacrifice For Four Policemen

During his thirty-seven years of life, Maurice Clemmons was an absolute wreckage of a man that liberty and freedom only intensified.

He was first arrested in Little Rock, Arkansas at the age of 17 on multiple burglary, assault, battery and robbery charges. He was arrested while he was a junior in high school for carrying a .25-caliber pistol on school property. He did not return to school following his expulsion to complete his education. By 1990, his sentencing amounted to an accumulated 108 years based on eight felony convictions.

On multiple occasions he exhibited unruly and violent behavior during court appearances. Each Clemmons appearance demanded extra security and in one instance, he was shackled in leg irons.

Throughout his problems, there were always rationales and excuses for seemingly incomprehensible behavior. He explained his gun charge as an excuse to protect him from bullying by d*opers*. His violent behavior directed towards law enforcement authorities was simply dismissed as immaturity.

In 1999, after serving ten years of his extended sentence, he filed a clemency appeal with Arkansas Governor Mike Huckabee. He drafted a fanciful letter taking full responsibility for his actions and attributing them again to immaturity, a lack of good influences and manipulations from the wrong sort of peer pressure. He claimed to have matured and changed his behavior during his incarceration. He stressed the excessive length of his sentence was unjust in proportion to the magnitude of his modest teenage indiscretions.

Huckabee reduced his sentence from the original 108 years to slightly over 47. In principle, this should have kept him in prison. The rationale for the sentence reduction was based on its excessive length and the age of the perpetrator when the crimes were committed. Clemmons written assurances of repentance apparently moved Huckabee. The prosecuting district attorney argued vehemently against the reduction.

Huckabee's decision enabled Clemmons' immediate parole consideration. The Arkansas Parole Board unanimously approved his release in the summer of 2000. The wait for his return to jail was brief. Clemmons violated parole by committing aggravated robbery and theft the following year in Ouachita County. He was convicted and sentenced to ten years, but bureaucratic wrangling by his lawyers got him released by 2004.

Clemmons had additional excuses explaining his antisocial behavior. He *wasn't ready* the first time he was released. He would continue to try and *do the right thing*. His later interpretation of the *right thing* would result in catastrophe.

The state of Arkansas solved their Maurice Clemmons problem by agreeing to his 2004 relocation to Washington. The burden for his erratic behavior and activities had now shifted halfway across the country.

Clemmons enjoyed his sole stretch of stability during the initial five years he resided in Tacoma. He operated a landscaping and power-washing business out of his house. During that period, he was reported to have purchased six houses, one located in Arkansas. Had the beast within finally been placated?

The answer became evident during four days in May 2009 when his reckless behavior and mental state returned. On May 9th, he was arrested for throwing rocks at neighborhood houses, cars and people. He punched the arresting sheriff's deputy in the face and fought belligerently with jail personnel. He was able to post a $40,000 bail bond and was released the next day.

On May 11th, his behavior further disintegrated and into extremes. His rantings became delusional. During the early morning of the following day, he appeared naked in his living room. He ordered two of his juvenile cousins to fondle him. They complied out of fear and by 4 a.m., he had gathered his entire family together including his common-law wife. He demanded that they strip naked together. He repeatedly referred to himself as Jesus. The circus was ready to spill out onto the streets.

It required nearly two months to formally investigate and arrest him for his lewd acts. His ravings worsened. The state of Arkansas did not want him returned and waved extradition rights, despite his parole violation.

During the next four months he was evaluated by court appointed psychologists to determine his sanity. Clemmons confessed to an assortment of hallucinations including graphic debaucheries, individuals drinking blood and eating babies. He identified himself as a direct relative to nearly every notable African-American of prominence. The extent of his confessions clearly indicated a man who had entirely lost his grip on reality and sanity.

After an exhaustive mental evaluation, the psychologists

concluded that Clemmons was competent to stand trial.

During this evaluation period, he remained free and at liberty. Just prior to his trial, he decided to commit his worse atrocity.

Clemmons failed to check in with his community corrections officer. On Thanksgiving Day, he cut off a GPS monitor that his bail bond company had secured to his ankle. There was no follow-up on either of these acts.

He spoke openly about gunning down people and particularly police officers to an assortment of friends and family. None of them took the slightest initiative to report the impending threat or avert disaster. He now considered himself Lucifer and contemplated how to eliminate the maximum number of police officers efficiently. He debated whether to simply invade a police station or telephone in a distress call and await the responding prey.

Impulsively on the morning of November 29, 2009 at around 8 a.m. he determined his method of attack. He passed by a coffee shop in Parkland where four officers were working on laptops before their shift. A friend, Darcus Allen was his transportation to the location and waited nearby.

Clemmons entered the cafe scarcely observed by the officers. He squared into position and meticulously fired at each. He killed all four with shots to the head. Slain were Mark Renninger, 39, Ronald Owens, 37, Tina Griswold, 40, and Greg Richards, 42. Richards managed to struggle with him at the restaurant doorway before succumbing to his bullet wounds. He shot the fleeing Clemmons in the back before he expired.

Clemmons was driven to his house and borrowed a car from one of his housemates. He specified that he'd been shot by police but didn't elaborate. He was on the run and needed immediate assistance. One of the Seattle-Tacoma regions fiercest manhunts followed. Assuming Clemmons would remain in the area, police shadowed potential sanctuary houses of his friends and family. Their efforts proved in vain as the killer seemingly vanished.

On December 1st, around 2:45 a.m. Clemmons' good fortune and vehicle stalled in a Rainier district neighborhood. He was idling his engine with its hood raised parked next to a sidewalk. A patrolling officer recognized the vehicle as having been reported stolen earlier.

Employing his most brazen tactic yet in a lifetime of incredulous behavior, Clemmons approached the officer as he was writing a report. The policeman immediately recognized the most wanted fugitive in the Pacific Coast and ordered him to stop and show his hands.

Clemmons had spent a lifetime failing to comply with authority. He attempted to flee around the disabled vehicle armed with a handgun that had belonged to one of the slain officers. He was unable to fire a shot.

The patrolman fired several rounds at him with two direct hits killing him. A later forensic disclosure indicated that the bullet Clemmons had sustained earlier from Officer Richards would have ultimately proved fatal. Another follow-up investigation determined that he had evaded the original dragnet by staying at an ex-girlfriend's house and then a South Seattle crack house, near where his car had broken down.

At the conclusion of the fiasco, it became evident that a volatile individual such as Maurice Clemmons should never have been a free man. A fractured legal system had completely exposed four police officers to a deadly menace.

Several members of Clemmons support system were arrested later on charges of providing knowingly misleading information to police and aiding and assisting his escape. A sister, aunt, cousin, ex-girlfriend and former employee were convicted. His brother was acquitted.

An obscene photo of a dead, nearly nude and bloated Maurice Clemmons was snapped and released publicly by an anonymous cell phone user. It remains disturbingly suspended in cyberspace for public viewing. His fatal bullet holes are visible.

In 2011, the driver from the Parkland killings, Darcus Allen, was convicted on four counts of first-degree murder for his role in shuttling Clemmons. The jury convicted him based on their confidence he had absolute knowledge of Clemmons' intentions. His protestations of ignorance were viewed as lies based on earlier statements he had made.

They had originally met as cellmates in Arkansas. He was sentenced to 420 years in prison and is currently interned at the Washington Corrections Center in Shelton. In a December 13, 2018 decision, the Washington Supreme Court ruled Allen would not face aggravated murder charges at his second upcoming trial. Although he was found guilty of first-degree murder at his first trial, they did not find him guilty of aggravating factors that would lead to an automatic sentence of life without parole. He will be facing still another trial on first-degree murder charges.

The coffee shop killing site has since been renamed Blue Steele Cafe. The café still services clientele and remains a memorial to the four slain officers. It is a testament to the sacrifice and often-unanticipated risk assumed by law enforcement personnel on a daily basis. The shop's reincarnation seems a fitting reminder for a multiple killing that should have never been allowed to occur.

Maurice Clemmons Killing Site:
Blue Steel Coffee Shop, 11401 South Steele Street, Lakewood

**Maurice Clemmons Death Site:
4422 South Kenyon Street, Seattle**

Niles Meservey Death: A Homicidal Impatience By One of the Good Guys

The motivation behind the fatal shooting of 51-year-old Niles Meservey on June 10, 2009 defied ethics. The subsequent legal travesty and wasted public expense that followed seemingly defied logic and justice.

Law enforcement officers share one of the most hazardous and thankless occupations in American communities. Each shift, they are required to adorn a figurative target on their back as they patrol and monitor streets and neighborhoods. Their performance expectations are often elevated beyond reasonable proportion. Their judgment is assumed to be impeccable and instantaneous. They are considered human but often not allowed human failings.

In short, they have a nearly impossible set of objectives every professional workday.

What transpired between Everett police officer Troy Meade and Niles Meservey raised a significant question as to the employment of appropriate restraint under confrontational circumstances.

Meade and another office arrived at the parking lot of a local tavern and encountered a suspected inebriated patron, Meservey, attempting to drive his vehicle home. The officers properly made attempts to disengage him from his car including two Taser jolts, but to no avail.

Meservey reportedly resisted their attempts and based on the officer's account spitefully attempted to reverse his car. An eyewitness indicated this action was due to him being boxed in. He did not demonstrate to the officer's satisfaction an intention towards calling for a taxi or transfer or listening to the officer's threats to arrest him. What followed seems unimaginable and callous.

At this stage in the standoff, the officers had multiple options to consider in stopping Meservey. Meade opted for the worst possible.

He raised and aimed his gun. He then fired deliberately into Meservey's back….seven times. The driver was killed instantly.

The Everett public became justifiably outraged over Meade's brazen impatience. Initially Everett's Police Chief ordered no internal investigation. Public pressure demanded an investigation. He relented.

The investigative findings presumably resulting in Meade's termination of employment due to unacceptable misconduct. The fired officer was given severance pay of nearly $184,000.

Meade was charged with second-degree murder and first-degree manslaughter. A jury acquitted him on the criminal charges. He was later found civilly responsible and the city of Everett settled with the victim's family for $500,000. The legal fees spent on defending Meade amounted to approximately $640,000. Meade currently represents himself as a truck driver for Waste Management.

It is stupefying to attempt to justify such arrogant behavior, violation of public trust and waste of public monies. Most Americans support the principles of law enforcement. They equally respect the dedicated individuals protecting and maintaining security under difficult circumstances.

One isolated officer's impulsive impatience undermined the credibility that police departments nationally are struggling to maintain. Most law enforcement agencies decry the unprecedented performance scrutiny they are currently under due to the proliferation of cell phone cameras and social media. In fairness however, this increasing media exposure of shoddy and sloppy operating procedures has showcased publicly an inefficiency that is sometimes criminal.

Many Americans, particularly with minority orientations, sense they are under direct assault by law enforcement agencies, the very institution they are supposed to respect. With each publicized violation and abuse, the public distrust widens the confidence gap.

The worse case scenario is that these offending officers may ultimately find reemployment in different jurisdictions one day. Their sins will be whitewashed and their incompetence intact.

**Niles Meservey Parking Lot Murder:
Former Chuckwagon Inn, 6720 Evergreen Way, Everett**

Timothy Brenton: A Police Officer Ambush Motivated By Extreme Hatred

Police officer Timothy Brenton was a nine-year veteran of the Seattle Police Department. He was assigned rookie officer Britt Sweeney as his partner. Her second evening of training was Halloween night, 2009. Both were seated in their parked patrol car following a routine traffic stop. They were reviewing the follow-up operational procedure in the volatile Central District of Seattle.

Out of nowhere, Christopher Monfort pulled his car up alongside and abruptly opened fire on both officers. Brenton, in the driver's seat was felled instantly with four bullets to the head. Sweeney in the resulting chaos, jumped out of the car preparing to return fire.

The killer had driven off into the night circling back in the direction he had arrived from.

Sweeney was disoriented and didn't realize her partner lay dead nearby. One of the bullets had grazed her head. She had the sensation of being hunted and ambushed and felt powerless. Her sole focus became survival. She did.

A public memorial service was held for Brenton on November 6th highlighted by a procession of police and fire vehicles throughout the city. On the same day, three law enforcement officials were closing in on a suspect in Tukwila. Christopher Monfort, 41, was the owner of a car that matched the description of the suspicious vehicle from the shooting scene. Officers confronted Monfort in the parking lot of his apartment complex.

He pulled a gun on the investigators and attempted to escape to his apartment. He was seriously outgunned and the pursuing officers opened fire seriously wounding him. He was treated at a nearby medical center. He was paralyzed from the waist down from the shooting.

In his apartment, police found three rifles, a shotgun, homemade explosives, booby traps and a barricade of tires. A ballistics examination from one of his rifles matched the bullets used in the earlier police assault.

Monfort posed a unique challenge for investigators to understand. He had no criminal record at the time of the killing and had graduated from the University of Washington studying law enforcement. Nine days before the shooting, he had set a fire and detonated pipe bombs that destroyed several police vehicles in the Charles Street maintenance yard.

Psychologists characterized Monfort as an extremist whose intense hatred of the police promoted him to wage a one-man terror crusade. His anger stemmed over his perceptions of injustices resulting from police brutality. His attorneys claimed that Monfort irrationally reasoned that if enough police officers were randomly killed, the deaths would reform their conduct and the department.

The therapist's arguments were an attempt to convince the jury of his insanity. The effect merely reinforced their certainty that he was sane and knew his actions were wrong. He simply didn't care. He had no prior acquaintance with Officers Brenton or Sweeney.

In 2015, he was convicted of murder, two counts of attempted murder and one count of arson. He was spared the death penalty and sentenced to life in prison. His spinal chord injury and paralysis made his sentence even more taxing given the accompanying chronic pain and constant battle with skin and urinary tract infections. His estimated incarcerated life expectancy was between nine and eighteen years. He shortened his sentence with a drug overdose on January 18, 2017 at the Washington State Penitentiary in Walla Walla. His toxicology test indicated that he died of acute amitriptyline intoxication. The drug is used to treat mental illness, including major depressive disorder.

To Britt Sweeney's credit and honor, she remained a police officer and is employed as part of the city's bicycle patrol. Her ability to recover from the extreme trauma and remain a contributing member of the police force is the sole illumination from a sad, twisted chronicle of misguided vengeance.

Seattle Police Officer Timothy Brenton Murder: Corner 29th and Yesler Way, Seattle

Officer Volney Stevens: An Open Season On Shooting Seattle Policemen

A simple abandoned vehicle call to the Ballard Police Station dispatched officer Volney Stevens and Sergeant Edward Herald to a remote stretch of 32nd Avenue in the Magnolia Bluff neighborhood on Friday morning, January 14, 1921. A car had been stranded for at least two days on a dirt stretch dead end near Smith Cove on Elliot Bay.

The car had been stolen and used previously in a string of burglaries from Bellingham to Enumclaw. Four men with a suitcase were roaming the area near the Howe Street Bridge. The caretaker of Carleton Park reported the suspicious group to the police. The four men, between the ages of 18-21 were Creighton Dodge, Ward Daniels, Louis Madsen and Clifford Brown.

In 1921, police cars did not have radio communications, so the two responding officers were unaware of the previous call regarding the foursome. By the time they arrived to inspect the stranded car, the men were seated inside and mulling over their predicament.

Around 9:00 a.m. Sergeant Edward Herald walked over to the car and immediately spied the suitcase. His intuition sensed something was wrong. He suspected it contained liquor or drugs. He inquired as to the contents. The group responded with silence. He lifted it out of the car and bent over to open and examine it. One of the four jumped out of the car and pointed a gun at Herald. He then disarmed him and shoved him into their vehicle.

During the sequence of events, Dodge and Daniels began shooting at Volney Stevens. He returned their fire. He hit

Dodge in the abdomen and Daniels in the arm. Amidst the gunfire exchange, Stevens was hit twice in the torso. He lay prone in the middle of the road. Herald remained a hostage and uninjured. Approximately twenty shots were exchanged.

The two contingents followed different paths. Herald rushed to assist Stevens. The gang sprinted to the police car and drove off. The caretaker who had telephoned police about the four suspicious individuals joined and assisted both officers until another car could transport Stevens to the hospital. Shortly past noon after undergoing surgery and blood transfusions, Volney Stevens died from his wounds with his wife by his side.

The fugitives were unable to escape far as the Ballard Bridge was raised. The Magnolia Park district is a residential peninsula. Once their water crossing access to downtown Seattle was blocked, they were trapped. They abandoned the stolen police car. On foot, they desperately knocked on the door of a residence and tried to convince the owner that two of them were sick and needed a place to remain. The 1920s was characterized as an age of innocence, but not necessarily blind ignorance.

Viewing the bleeding of the wounded men, there were two accounts of the owner's reaction. In one, she slammed the door in their face and immediately telephoned police. In the other she invited them to rest and alerted a neighbor to telephone the police. Whatever account proved accurate, the men didn't linger and instead returned to a nearby beach to steal a 20-foot rowboat.

By the time they had shoved off onto the frigid waters headed towards downtown, police officers had arrived on the shoreline. They fired warning shots and ordered the four to return. The prospect of a prison term or death by gunshot and a January bath in Salmon Bay became elemental. They rowed back 150 feet and were arrested.

Creighton Dodge, who was wounded in the gunfire exchange, would die from an infection following surgery five days later. Daniels, Madsen and Brown were tried and sentenced to life in prison, serving their terms at the State Penitentiary in Walla Walla.

Daniels and two other convicts would escape in 1925 and go on another crime spree for a month before their capture in Eugene, Oregon. He was again returned to Walla Walla but not for long. Between 1927-29, Washington Governor Roland Hartley paroled the three surviving members of the gang.

On January 21, 1921, only one week after Steven's murder, a single suspect would shoot three additional Seattle policemen to death. It appeared to be open season on killing law enforcement officers.

There is a popular notion that during this era, the citizenry, elected officials and judicial bodies revered law officers with greater fidelity than today. The assumption may be true, but it may equally be simple mythology. Police work has eternally been unpredictable, sometimes thankless and always dangerous.

Public and political outrage is not always measured and vented in consistent doses.

**Officer Volney Stevens Shootout Murder:
32nd Avenue West and West Galer Street**

Below Magnolia Bluff and Entrance to Elliot Bay, Seattle

Otto Zehm: An Overzealous Killing of A Simple Man

Otto Zehm was a simple man with a predictable routine. He was diagnosed as developmentally disabled. He worked as a Spokane based janitor. He did not own a car. As was his habit, he regularly visited his bank's ATM to withdraw small amounts of money from his account. He would then walk to a nearby convenience store and purchase a soft drink and fast food. Zehm reportedly rarely varied his routine.

March 18, 2006 was simply another workday, ATM and convenience store visit for Zehm. However on this day, two young women mistakenly thought he was attempting to steal money from the ATM. In their zeal, they telephoned a police dispatcher and relayed his movements via their vehicle.

Zehm entered the convenience store and gravitated towards the soft drink section to select a soda. The first of two responding officers who arrived at the scene, Karl Thompson immediately approached a startled Zehm whose back was initially turned. Thompson ordered him to release the soft drink. Unsatisfied by Zehm's immediate response in very constrained space, he then batoned Zehm to the ground. He struck him seven times including multiple blows to the head.

As if this violation of police procedure was not sufficient, Zehm was tasered sixteen seconds later. He was then hogtied and placed on his stomach for more than sixteen minutes. As the beatings and abuse continued, five additional members of the Spokane Police force arrived. None intervened to protect him.

Reports indicated that one of the officers requested a *non-*

rebreather mask from paramedics at the scene and strapped it to Zehm's face. The mask was not attached to an oxygen tank. Three minutes later, Zehm stopped breathing and elemental overzealous police response turned into a homicide. Zehm was declared brain dead two days later due to a lack of oxygen.

The travesty did not end with Zehm's killing. A shameful departmental cover-up followed. The first official police version brazenly indicated that Zehm had lunged at Thompson with his plastic soft drink bottle. The store's surveillance camera portrayed a contrary version. As Thompson barked verbal orders to Zehm and raised his baton to strike, the victim merely backed away slowly.

The internal investigation moved at a glacial pace. The results proved publicly unsatisfactory. Only three of the seven officers involved in the attack received any punishment. This amounted to a single official day of administrative paid leave. The department was clearly intent to weather public criticism for such a heinous act. They almost succeeded.

Public opinion however did not entirely subside. Several diverse organizations and individuals sustained outrage, protests and public challenges. Nearly a year and a half later, a group of 200 diverse protestors gathered and approached the Spokane City Council. They outlined demands for more intense scrutiny and independent oversight of Spokane Police Department operations.

Their efforts were stimulated by an earlier Independence Day arrest of protestors at the local Riverfront Park. The Zehm case was prominent amongst their concerns. Their ranks were diverse, but the impact contributed to later action.

One can easily imagine the magnitude of the national media exposure and amplification of protest had this been a racial killing. Otto Zehm however was a simple, nearly forgotten man with few proponents. His story might symbolically represent many of us violated under identical circumstances.

On June 22, 2009, over three years after the killing, a federal Grand Jury handed down an indictment on Officer Karl Thompson. The charges were based on his unreasonable use of force and making a false entry into a record being investigated by a federal agency. His trial began in October 2011 after being relocated to Yakima. His attorneys raised concerns about the adverse Spokane media coverage, which might affect his defense.

A jury found this argument irrelevant and convicted Thompson on both counts. An estimated fifty police officers were attendance and saluted Thompson as a show of solidarity. It was the sort of symbolic gesture that further erodes public confidence in law enforcement ethics.

Thompson's attorneys argued for a minimal sentence. Instead he received 51 months, which under the circumstances was probably the maximum possible given his professional background. He was released from the Federal Correctional Institution in Safford, Arizona in February, 2016 after serving a four-year sentence. He was paid his salary during his imprisonment and received his full police pension upon his release.

This expense has been exasperated to extremes. Washington State paid over $500,000 to his legal defense team. The City of Spokane reached a settlement accompanied by a public apology with the family of Otto

Zehm for $1.67 million. There have been zero published statements of contrition by Thompson or the six officers present during the act. The moment for ethical contemplation and redemption passed nearly a decade ago.

There is no singular aspect in this tragedy that uplifts. The two young women who erroneously targeted Zehm were never identified. They have only their conscience to haunt them. There was never a public mention of the witnessing convenience store employee contradicting the initial sanctioned police version. The police department, which initially attempted to stonewall the facts and then reluctantly cooperated, did little to restore public trust in their integrity.

In the end, it was a mounted convenience store surveillance camera that convicted Thompson and all organized attempts to cover up the indecent act. The video streams and remains online for public consumption…if you can stomach the footage.

**Otto Zehm's Murder Site:
Zip Trip Market, 1712 N. Division, Spokane**

Donna Perry: Assigning Gender Accountability For Past Sins

Does gender orientation affect criminality and aggressive tendencies? Is reinvention by surgical procedure a legitimate defense strategy?

Based on Donna Perry's 2014 Spokane arraignment and the accompanying media coverage, one might assume that violence and murder are exclusively male genetic traits. In 2000, she underwent transgender surgery in Thailand. She claimed to investigators that the surgery made her a different person from her previous violent alter ego, Douglas Perry. The sex change operation eradicated the violent rage that had dominated her previous existence.

This anger was manifested into the brutal shooting deaths of at least three prostitutes Yolana Sapp, Kathleen Brisbois and Nickie Lowe. Each was discovered nude along the banks of the Spokane River in 1990. The murderer police sought was identified as the .22-caliber killer based on the employed weapon of death.

Perry was linked to the killings and crime scene via DNA matching of her fingerprints after being arrested in 2014 on federal weapons charges.

Donna, now 67, alleged she *has killed nobody*. She was not responsible for the acts of her past persona, Douglas. She could no longer remember what actions he might have committed with the passage of time.

The resolution over Perry's claim has been debated in evaluating the effects of hormone therapy. Can surgical procedures play a role in diminishing aggression? The practice bears a resemblance to chemical castration, a controversial procedure used with sex offenders. The long-term results have been inconclusive.

Donna's naming confusion created initially a dilemma for her legal representation since they were officially unable to meet and prepare a defense. Donna was still designated as *Douglas* in the county records. Donna has steadfastly refused to stand trial for the crimes she maintains were the fault of her prior male personage.

For a period of time, her strategy succeeded in delaying her trial.

Slightly built and grey haired, she had generated international press attention for her plight. Does a fresh identity exempt her from past transgressions or is she merely employing a desperate defense strategy? Contemporary society is in the midst of an extended discussion over what is considered *normal* with transgender identities. Socially, many advocates consider the issue as essential Civil Rights.

The tricky question emerges in distancing from one's past.

Can individuals undergo a radical sex change transformation and relieve themselves of prior accountabilities? The issue could create a dangerous precedent.

For Donna Perry, in July 2017 her charade was rudely terminated. Entering the courthouse, she smiled and engaged in small talk with her appointed attorneys. Scanning the courtroom filled with friends and family of the victims, she lightheartedly queried: *What do we got here? Bad news?*

The question couldn't have proven more understated. Douglas or Donna if you prefer was sentenced to three consecutive life sentences without the possibility of parole. The perpetrator was then lashed and lacerated by the words and tears of those that suffered from the callous murders.

Indeed the news couldn't have been worse. Donna Perry got her partial wish. She is now incarcerated at the Washington Corrections Center for Women in Gig Harbor, but her loss of freedom will remain permanent.

**Donna (Douglas) Perry's Residence:
2006 East Empire Avenue, Spokane**

Kathleen Brisbois Murder Site: Spokane River: Trent Avenue and Pines Road, Spokane

Nickie Lowe Murder Site: 3200 Block of South Riverton, Spokane

Yolanda Sapp's Murder Site: 4100 Block of East Upriver Drive, Spokane

George Russell, Jr.: Outsider and Sadistic Serial Killing

Estrangement was a common thread throughout George Russell's formation. He was alienated from his family, his peers and authority figures.

He was the consummate outsider; superficially liked by many but understood by no one. He was abandoned at six-months old with a negligent grandmother on the East Coast. His presence was inconvenient and barely tolerated when reunited with his mother and new stepfather on affluent Mercer Island. He was in the way with her new life and in competition with the younger daughter the couple had together.

Russell became one of the few African-American residents on the island. He parlayed this distinction into manipulative relationships. He understood early that being perceived as *unique* necessitated being clever, charming and somewhat flamboyant. Respecting laws and rules were meant for others.

George Russell Jr. understood the value of flattery, persuasion and staging the role of victim based on his skin color. He groveled up to local law enforcement authorities by becoming useful. He ran errands on their behalf and worked as an informant.

He needed their patronage as he was habitually in trouble for stealing and petty theft. His abuses and offenses were often dismissed as harmless adolescent behavior. Russell was considered amusing because he could pathologically lie to ingratiate himself. The outsider within in seethed inside.

His boldness and depravity escalated. Dressed in dark

clothing, he began invading homes, even as families slept inside. He sensed himself invisible. He lifted cash, jewelry and their personal mementos. More disturbingly, he cultivated a fascination towards voyeurism. He would obsessively hover and admire women sleeping inside, unaware of his presence.

None of his acquaintances could imagine the fermenting evil within him. He was a classical sociopath and could assimilate socially. Even if he did periodically confess his transgressions to his friends, they dismissed them as George's exaggerations.

He became a fixture at Bellevue's nightclubs. He would exaggerate his sexual exploits, troll for partners incessantly and tote around a canvas bag loaded with pornographic magazines. He couldn't maintain a job and fabricated stories of employment with the police department as an undercover agent. He remained amusing company but his inconsistencies became blatant. By the age of 31, he had been incarcerated twenty-four times for petty offenses.

His lethal perversions began to overwhelm his sense of restraint.

During the summer of 1990, suburban and opulent Bellevue was riveted by the discovery of two ritualistically slain young women. The killings were sadistic and the bodies posed in macabre positions.

Mary Ann Pohlreich was stabbed to death and laid carefully nude beside a fast food restaurant dumpster during early morning hours. She had been viciously beaten to death and posed to resemble lying within a coffin. The vicious murder showed no signs of sexual violation.

The second killing was more excessive. Carol Marie Bleethe was forcefully battered to death in her own bed while asleep. Her two young daughters were at home during the slaying but heard nothing. The killing was ghastly and her body violated with orifices.

On September 3rd, Andrea Levine was savagely beaten in her sleep and again her body arranged in a degrading position. The two latter victims had been sexually violated after their killings.

The crime scenes left significant DNA evidence. The patterns behind the last two appeared similar. The intruder in both killings was practiced in the art of unobserved household entry.

Russell initially offered his assistance to his police contacts in the investigation. Soon however, his bizarre enthusiasm and freshly discovered evidence cast him as a primary suspect. A former girlfriend informed police of her suspicions.

Too many forensic and circumstantial clues pointed towards him. Blood type and hair samples on the dead bodies were identical matches. The investigation concluded by Russell being arrested for the murders. The killings ceased.

His circle of acquaintances were shocked by his arrest. Many found the seemingly harmless and jovial George an incredulous suspect for such violent and excessive acts.

At his trial, forensic and psychological profile experts exhaustively constructed the common denominators behind the three killings. Russell observed the proceedings as a detached and often bored observer. He did not take the stand in his own defense.

The jury rendered first-degree murder convictions against him for all three women's deaths. He was sentenced to life in prison without the possibility of parole. He is currently incarcerated at the Stafford Creek Corrections Center after a stint at the Clallam Bay Corrections Center.

Understanding the motives behind George Russell, Jr.'s acts invites imaginative psychological speculation.

Did he simmer with antisocial anger surrounded by wealth and acceptance he found impossible to obtain? What ultimately propelled him into violent and ritualistic homicide may never be adequately explained or rationalized.

With a classical sociopath, truth and clarity behind their motives is often as ambiguous as their personal perceptions of estrangement. George Russell, Jr. never confessed his guilt or motivations. He will perish with his secrets and demons.

Mary Ann Pohlreich: McDonald's Dumpster, 1401 156th Avenue NE, Bellevue

Andrea *Randi* Levine's Residence: 2064 NE 89th Avenue, Bellevue

Gary Ridgway: The Green River Executioner Appearing As Evil Incarnate

If the devil assumed an earthly identity, he could find no more appropriate persona than Gary Leon Ridgway. Known better in popular culture as the Green River Killer, Ridgway by his own admission lost track in totaling the number of his victims. He confessed to 71 murders, was convicted of 49 and was presumed to have killed in excess of 90+.

When man can longer tabulate the death and misery he has spread to humanity, the question immediately surfaces as to what purpose is his continued living?

Prosecutors made a plea bargain with the devil in granting him a life prison sentence without parole instead of a death sentence. Should such an offer be upheld to a man who has disregarded and disdained society's rules throughout his life? Are we obliged to respect our agreements with Satan?

Ridgway was born the second of three boys in Salt Lake City, Utah. His IQ was measured at 82, signifying below average intelligence and he correspondingly did poorly in school. The seeds of his future sexual perversity were accentuated by his mother's actions. She would bathe him while he was naked at fourteen after having wet his bed.

At 16, he stabbed a six-year-old boy in the woods to experience what it would be like to kill someone. The victim survived.

Ridgway didn't graduate from high school until he was 20 and married his first wife upon graduation. He enlisted in the Navy and was sent to Vietnam. He served on board a supply ship and saw combat. In Vietnam, he began his sexual obsession of having intercourse with prostitutes. His wife had an extramarital affair and his marriage ended within a year.

He would marry on two additional occasions, with both relationships ending because of infidelities by both partners. During his second marriage, he assumed another preoccupation with religious fanaticism, becoming a devout church attendee and proselytizing door-to-door.

His sexual mania plagued him with an insatiable appetite. Sex became his absorption. His three wives and several ex-girlfriends could not satisfy his urges, so he renewed his employment of prostitutes. Warfare was fermenting within his soul based on the conflict between his religious beliefs, his uncontrollable lusts and his disgust for women selling sexual services.

Between 1982 and 1984, a majority of his murders were initiated along the Pacific Highway South (currently International Boulevard). This area of Sea-Tac then was in the process of major reconstruction to accommodate the expansion of the Seattle-Tacoma International Airport. Prostitutes proliferated the construction zone and made Ridgway's search for victims simplistic.

Young women, both professionals and transients, lined the boulevard. Through Ridgway's eyes, their role was for his use and then disposal. He was gratified by a sexual release he was not obliged to pay for and the excitement generated by strangling his victims and concealing their bodies. He was reported in several instances to return to the dumping sites and engage in sex with the cadavers.

Many of the bodies were dumped in clusters in secluded wooded areas around the Green River, not far from their original pick-up location. Ridgway was known for contaminating his disposal sites with gum, cigarettes and written notes from other individuals to confuse police.

His *Green River* designation was thrust upon him after his initial victims were discovered floating atop a winding river stretch under Kent's Meeker Street Bridge. Most of the women he killed were strangled from behind in his truck, home or secluded areas that he had transported them.

In 1984, at the height of his rampage, incarcerated serial killer Ted Bundy was consulted to offer his opinions into the psychology and behavior of the killer. Bundy correctly suggested that the perpetrator would return to his dumpsites to have sex with his victims. It was a practice he had employed.

Ridgway was arrested twice in 1982 and 2001 on prostitution solicitation charges. He became a prime suspect in 1983 for the Green River killings but erroneously passed a polygraph test the following year. The police and FBI continued to monitor his activities and in 1987 acquired his hair and saliva samples.

Ridgway began dating his eventual third wife in 1985 and they married in 1988. As a published suspect in the killings, he was forced to move from a residence in Kent and relocate to SeaTac. Forensics technology was improving and the increased sophistication would ultimately connect Ridgway.

During the dating period with his wife and even throughout their marriage, his killings continued, but at a declining rate. In November 2001, police finally arrested him at a Renton truck factory where he was employed as a spray painter. DNA evidence conclusively linked semen left in four victims to the saliva swab sampling acquired in 1987. Spray paint spheres from his truck factory were linked to three other victims.

The devil had been cornered and captured, but had one negotiating chip remaining to spare his life. Prosecutors were uncertain they could deliver a death penalty verdict based on the evidence they had acquired on these seven deaths. They were also uncertain as to the exact number of fatalities Ridgway was responsible for. He was the lone individual who could confirm the grisly count.

On November 5, 2003, Ridgway pleaded guilty to 48 charges of aggravated first-degree murder. In return, he was promised that he would be spared execution in exchange for his cooperation in locating the remains of his victims and providing other pertinent details.

Ridgway was sentenced to 48 life sentences with no possibility of parole and an additional 10 years for tampering with evidence. Ridgway led prosecutors to three bodies in 2003 and stretched out his confessional process to over five months of interviews. He hedged and was evasive on numerous specific details and altered his stories periodically to extend the process. He was in no hurry to return to solitary confinement at the Washington State Penitentiary in Walla Walla.

The list of his victims remains sobering reading accompanied by their age. The sheer horror of so many faceless deaths is matched only by the prospect of how many were never revealed. Each woman had a name and identity. Each woman had a life. Ridgway stole theirs. Over the next decade, hikers and random individuals would discover some of their remains, unaware of the significance.

The names of his confirmed dead include:

1982: Wendy Lee Coffield (16). Gisele Ann Lovvorn (17), Debra Lynn Bonner (23), Marcia Fay Chapman (31). Cynthia Jean Hinds (17). Opal Charmaine Mills (16), Terry Rene Milligan (16), Mary Bridget Meehan (18), Debra Lorraine Estes (15), Linda Jane Rule (16), Denise Darcel Bush (23), Shawnda Leea Summers (16), Shirley Marie Sherrill (18), Rebecca Marrero (20), Colleen Renee Brockman (15) and Sandra Denise Major (20).

1983: Delores LaVerne Williams (17), Gail Lynn Mathews (23). Andrea Childers (19), Sandra Kay Gabbert (17), Kimi-Kai Pitsor (16), Marie Malvar (18). Carol Ann Christensen (21), Martina Theresa Authorlee (18), Cheryl Lee Wims (18), Yvonne Shelly Antosh (19), Carrie Ann Rois (15), Constance Elizabeth Naon (19), Kelly Marie Ware (22), Tina Marie Thompson (21), April Dawn Buttram (16), Debbie May Abernathy (26), Tracy Ann Winston (19), Maureen Sue Feeney (19), Mary Sue Bello (25), Pammy Annette Avent (15), Delise Louise Plager (22), Kimberly Nelson (21), Lisa Yates (19) and Jane Doe B-10.

1984: Mary Exzetta West (16), Cindy Anne Smith (17) and Jane Doe B-17.

1986: Patricia Michelle Barczak (19).

1987: Roberta Joseph Hayes (21).

1990: Marta Reeves (36).

1993: Jane Doe B-20.

1998: Patricia Yellowrobe (38).

Ridgeway was suspected of, but not charged with the murders of Tammy Vincent (17), Amina Agisheff (35), Kase Ann Lee (16), Tammie Liles (16), Kelly Kay McGinniss (18), Angela Marie Girdner (16) and Patricia Osborn (19).

He was also considered a person of interest in several other disappearances and murders, not originally attributed to the Green River Killer. The women included Martha Morrison (17), Kristi Lynn Vorak (13), Patricia Ann Leblanc (15), Darci Warde (16), Cora McGuirk (22) and an unidentified African-American woman who disappeared in December 1980.

Numerous mentions of Ridgway's terror have been exploited in various medias, music, art and literature. The macabre nature of his killings and number of his victims has repulsed popular culture to the identical degree it has fascinated.

On May 14, 2015, Ridgway was transferred from the Washington State Penitentiary to the USP Florence, a high-security federal prison east of Canon City, Colorado. The intent was to remove him from isolation and rejoin the general prison population. His access to convicted killers might have proven an ideal opportunity for one of them to gain public notoriety via his murder.

The experiment was abandoned after five months due to an intense public outcry against the transfer. The Washington Corrections Secretary announced in a face saving gesture that Ridgway would be returned to the Washington State Penitentiary in Walla Walla to be *easily accessible* for open murder investigations.

In all negotiations and compromises with the devil, no one ultimately comes out appearing sanitized.

Green River Killer's Bus Shelter Pick Up Point:
14100 Block of International Boulevard, Tukwilla

**Meeker Street Bridge Crossing the Green River:
2000 West Meeker Street Block, Kent**

**Gary Ridgway's (Green River Killer) Residences:
4633 S. 348th Street, Auburn**

2139 S. 253rd Street, Kent

21859 32nd Pl S, SeaTac

The Fatal Curse of Jake Bird

Jake Bird was a serial killer anomaly. Reportedly born in Louisiana in 1901 in a location he claimed to have forgotten, Bird was a 45-year-old African American transient convicted of rape and murder. He understood, before it became common practice, that the strategic filing of appeals and exaggerated death claims could delay his ultimate execution.

The *Tacoma Ax-Killer* was best known for a curse he inflicted upon law enforcement and judicial personnel during his final response statements after being condemned to death.

Bird was convicted of raping and murdering Bertha Kludt and her teenage daughter Beverly June on October 30, 1947. Screams were initially heard coming from the house by neighbors. As police approached, they viewed a barefoot Bird fleeing the house and crashing through a front yard picket fence. He was cornered into a nearby alley and forcibly subdued by officers after brandishing a switchblade knife.

His clothes were drenched with blood and brain matter due to the savagery of the attacks. In his confession, he indicated his intention was simply to burglarize the house. He claimed to have killed Bertha Kludt who had discovered his presence and tried to stop him while he was attempting to flee. Her daughter was killed when she came to her mother's aid.

Investigators found his story preposterous considering the axe had come from an adjacent shed and he was barefoot. Bird had an extensive criminal record of burglary, attempted murder and a total of 31 years of incarceration in three states. Police speculated that he had entered the house to sexually assault Bertha Kludt. He murdered her daughter when she tried to flee. When not incarcerated, Bird worked as a railroad gandy, laying and maintaining tracks. His railroad employment kept him moving regularly.

At his trial, he was charged with the premeditated first-degree murder of Bertha Kludt, which qualified him for the death penalty. He was not charged for the murder of Beverly June. He pled not guilty and recanted an earlier confession, which he claimed had been beaten out of him by the police. The judge allowed the confession to be submitted as evidence.

The trial lasted two and a half days. The jury required 35 minutes to deliver their verdict and recommended the death penalty. Given an opportunity to address the courtroom following the sentencing, Bird maximized the opportunity. He was furious that the judge had denied him the opportunity to represent himself. He was certain that his own legal counsel was conspiring against him.

He addressed the assemblage: *I'm putting the Jake Bird hex on all of you who had anything to do with my being punished. Mark my words you will die before I do.*

Such words might be easily dismissed in the passion of the moment. They proved prophetic.

His judge, Edward Hodge died of a heart attack within a month of Bird's curse, as did one of the police officers that had recorded his initial confession. An officer involved in his second confession, the court's chief clerk, a prison guard and one of his lawyers died within a year of his sentencing. Coincidence or curse?

If there remained the slightest doubt regarding the guilt of Jake Bird, certainty was confirmed during his subsequent appeals. Condemned to a death scheduled for January 16, 1948, he claimed responsibility for another 44 murders. He volunteered his assistance with police to solve these open cases.

He was granted a 60-day reprieved by Washington governor Monrad Wallgren. Police from eleven states converged and confirmed his responsibility in eleven deaths He proved knowledgeable enough about another 33 to be considered a primary suspect. His primary weapon was generally an axe or hatchet. He had a disposition towards Caucasian women.

Similar to many subsequent serial killers, Bird realized that the more details he revealed, the longer his lifespan was extended. He survived another eighteen months of incarceration until his final petitions to State, Federal and the United States Supreme Courts were denied. His violent legacy culminated with a noose.

He was hung shortly after midnight on July 15, 1949. There were 125 witnesses. No further Jake Bird hexes were reported. The subsequent longevity of those in attendance remains unconfirmed.

There are many who scoff at the notion and legitimacy of hexes and haunting. Over seventy years following the slaying of Bertha Kludt and her daughter, their house and shed remains as uninhabitable in August 2019 as it did four years earlier. It has been repainted and cosmetically upgraded, but to little avail. If indeed Jake Bird sealed the earthly fate of his emissaries of doom, so too has he cursed the site of his final killing.

**Bertha Kludt's Murder Site in 2015 (Jake Bird):
1007 South 21st Street, Tacoma**

(2015)

(2019)

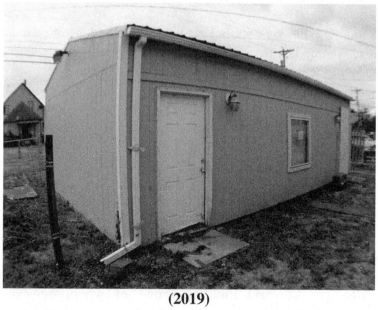
(2019)

The Vile Pride of Child Killer Joe Kondro

Every parent shares a common fear of child abduction by strangers. For decades, impressionable children have been warned against the dangers of accepting gifts or rides from individuals they do not know. Rima Traxler's parents took precautions even further by warning their daughter to avoid anyone unless they knew a special password.

What her parents and 8 year-old Rima didn't realize was that a close family friend, *Uncle Joe* Kondro, then 25, was the very child predator they most feared.

On May 15, 1985, Kondro told Rima that he'd been sent by her parents to pick her up and drive her to a nearby swimming hole. Earlier that very day, he had been drinking beers with her stepfather, a high school classmate, on their porch. Both of them had been teasing Rima's mother as she mowed the lawn.

Rima Traxler was strangled, her body hidden and never discovered. The mystery behind her disappearance festered in Longview for twelve years without resolution.

At the time, Joe Kondro was perhaps the last individual anyone would have suspected.

Kondro was a petty thief, thug and drug addict. Most people erroneously considered him merely self-destructive, but harmless. Over time, he was revealed to be an unrepentant killer and child molester. He'd been in drug rehabilitation programs and served jail time for auto theft, domestic violence, driving under the influence, forgery and drug dealing. He was reported to have been responsible for siring six to eight children, none of whom he ever financially supported.

The warning signs regarding his behavior were blatant, but he was simply dismissed as *Uncle Joe with a drinking problem*.

His homicidal instincts resurfaced (at least officially) on November 21, 1996. He picked up Kara Rudd, who'd decided to avoid school that day. Kara was a friend of one of Kondro's daughter. He had grown up with her mother and had previously lived with her family in their garage. Often inebriated and then threatening to Kara and her two siblings, Kondro was tolerated for eight months. He was asked to leave by Kara's mother, but remained on good terms with the family.

Kara asked Joe if he would drive her to a local pig farm, unaware that he harbored resentment towards her for his living quarters expulsion.

Instead of driving to the requested destination, he steered his vehicle to a notorious abandoned cabin near a popular swimming hole. He convinced or forced Kara into the small dwelling, then raped her. To conceal the violation, he choked her to death. It was never determined if his actions were premeditated or spontaneous. Kondro then drove to the nearby Mount Solo area and stuffed her body beneath an abandoned car that had been left stripped.

He assumed, possibly based on precedence, that if her body was never recovered, it would prove impossible to trace the killing to him.

The same day of the killing, he stopped by Kara's residence and was greeted by her distraught mother. Kondro acted concerned and had the audacity to drive her to the Longview police station to file a missing persons report.

Kondro's overconfidence failed him when Kara's partially clad body was discovered six weeks later. He became the immediate prime suspect. He was already in jail facing charges of witness tampering and first-degree child rape and molestation of three girls between the ages of 7 and 10.

For two years, Kondro refused to cooperate with investigators despite overwhelming DNA evidence linking him on Kara's body. He delayed, hoping to strike an advantageous bargain and avoid a potential death sentence. Finally, Kondro confessed to Kara Rudd's murder and supplied details behind Rima Traxler's strangulation.

Observers found it difficult to conclude that a predator and child killer such as Kondro would remain dormant twelve years between murders. Conclusive evidence was unable to link him to further crimes. He became the prime suspect in the stabbing and asphyxiation murder of another friend's daughter, Chila Silvernails of Kalama in 1982.

Kondro was convicted and received a 55-year sentence to life with no possibility of parole. It was the best deal he could negotiate. He remained mute regarding other disappearances potentially attributed to him,

In a 2006 newspaper interview with *The Daily News*, Kondro provided a chilling insight into the calloused mindset of a child serial killer. In the article, he flagrantly boasted of his luring tactics, abduction practices and additional exploits without providing traceable names.

His most stark revelation was his absolute absence of remorse. He maintained that he would have continued to kill had he not been apprehended. He cited the discovery of Rudd's body simply as *unfortunate* luck.

Kondro died during May 2012 at the State Penitentiary in Walla Walla of natural causes. Few mourned the loss. For the families he victimized, if a hell exists, their only consolation may be that Kondro will be roasting prominently in its molten core.

Hillside Burial Grounds

Germany Creek Swimming Hole

Abandoned Cabin Germany Creek

Lee Malvo: An Assassination Dictated By Subservience

The brutal shooting of Keenya Cook is a forgotten footnote from the more notorious Beltway Sniper killing spree that terrorized the Washington D.C. metropolitan region for over eight months in 2002. Those ten killings and three woundings were cowardly, unconscionable and the product of two men, John Allen Muhammad and Lee Boyd Malvo.

The elder and principle marksman, Muhammad was executed by lethal injection on November 11, 2009 in Virginia. He professed his innocence until his death, offering no final words or explanations for his actions.

The pair's legacy of violence would begin on February 16, 2002 at a hillside residence in East Tacoma. Traveling between Washington State and D.C. afterwards via southern states, the pair would kill another seven while wounding seven more in a blood rage that defied clear explanation.

The sequence of killings began as a bungled revenge murder. It became the sole homicide that was accompanied by a plausible motive.

John Muhammad had instructed Malvo to kill the best friend of his ex-wife. She had assisted his former spouse's escape from their abusive relationship. The murder was intended as repayment for her aid.

Malvo's relationship with Muhammad has long been scrutinized extensively. Malvo claimed that his older accomplice exerted a Machiavellian influence over him that was punctuated by a pattern of sexual abuse. He followed instructions without question or conscience.

Malvo botched the instruction by shooting the first person that answered his knock. Keenya Cook, 21, was the niece of the intended victim, living at the residence in the midst of sorting out her own life. She was in the process of undressing her baby daughter for a bath while preparing food on the kitchen stove. She had just broken up with her child's father and had moved in with her aunt and cousin. She managed a woman's clothing store.

The gunshot to her head was fatal and Malvo fled the scene. Investigators and family were baffled by an absence of motive. It wasn't until Muhammad and Malvo's later apprehension that the killing was linked directly to the pair. Malvo confessed, while Muhammad remained defiantly silent.

Malvo's role in the overall commission of the travesties has never been entirely substantiated. The manipulation by his mentor became obvious after extensive questioning and interrogation. Malvo original confessions were accentuated by inappropriate laughter. He made the disputable claim to being the sole triggerman in all of the sniper shootings. He later recanted his confession diminishing his role to that as the spotter. Given Muhammad's prior military background and Malvo's lack of training, his second version seemed more credible.

Malvo claimed that he had been instructed to claim sole responsibility for the shootings from the beginning to spare Muhammad a death penalty sentence. As a 16 year-old minor at the time of the killings, the likelihood of his receiving capital punishment was remote.

During his May 2006 trial, his attorneys attempted to parlay his subservient role into a plea of insanity based on his diminished capacity. They maintained his extreme mental and emotional imbalance made it impossible for him to distinguish right from wrong. Even as his secondary role became apparent, his continued accompaniment and assistance with Muhammad made evasion of responsibility impossible to accept by a jury.

Malvo continued to stress his marginal role in the killings and spun more elaborate and detailed versions of the pair's plans. Many of his claims appeared incredulous. Their multi-phased intent involved plans to gravitate from daily killings to extorting millions of dollars from the U.S. government.

Improbable as the scheme appeared, these monies would be used to finance coordinated paramilitary operations. The pair intended to recruit orphaned boys from Canada and train them as assassins to propagate a new Utopian society.

In the end, Malvo received multiple first-degree murder convictions that will incarcerate him permanently without the possibility of parole. He is currently interned at the Red Onion State Prison in Pound, Virginia. The facility is designated as a Supermax security prison housing 848 inmates and considered one of the toughest national institutions with stringent controls.

Two films and one television movie have portrayed the D.C. Sniper's exploits. Numerous media exposés have attempted to piece coherence into the pair's monstrous disregard for humanity. Malvo has periodically attempted to shed light into the unimaginable darkness behind their thinking.

Keenya Cook's legacy remains essentially forgotten, except for the heartbreak and loss endured by her family. In an attempt to rebuild her life, she had enrolled in local business courses to pursue her dream of one day owning a restaurant.

Lee Malvo was never tried nor will be for her killing. He will have multiple decades to contemplate the enormity of his actions. None of it may ever make sense.

Keenya Cook Murder Site (Lee Boyd Malvo): 2054 East 34th Street, Tacoma

Morris Frampton: The Beast and the Banality of Darkness

The violence and ferocity behind two killings in the summer of 1977 bore such a striking resemblance, detectives from two separate Seattle jurisdictions teamed up to track the murderer.

In July 1977, prostitute Iantha Buchanan Peters was savagely killed at a Seattle construction site. She had suffered massive trauma from multiple beatings. Her skull had been crushed and she had been strangled. The killer had violently yanked her skirt over her body and face. Her shirt had been ripped open. Her legs were spread and genitals fully exposed. The provocative pose was intended to shock. The image succeeded and remained burned into the memory of investigators.

Nine days later, another prostitute, Rosemary Stuart was found naked on a sloping hillside bank adjacent to the South Park Marina near the Admiralty Bridge. She had been beaten 81 times and savagely raped. She was left in a similarly vulnerable and unsettling pose. The difference with this killing was the existence of a neighborhood witness. She was awoken during the night hearing a woman crying, moaning and emitting sexual noises.

She insisted that two individuals might have been involved based on an overheard conversation and the sound of two car doors slamming before a vehicle drove off. She didn't call the police but came forward once she heard a body had been discovered. Her account of two male participants not one has never been substantiated.

The similarities and close spacing of the killings made assuming each were from the identical source almost obvious. Both crime sites yielded substantial clues. In particular, at the South Park crime scene, the killer had left tire impressions, a spilt yellow foam substance and his hastily fleeing car had clipped a post while exiting.

Working together, the two Seattle departments quickly arrested a suspect.

On the night of the killing, a Seattle gas station attendant had noticed very unusual details about a vehicle and the owner he was servicing. The driver had blood all over him. He used the restroom to wash himself. A taillight was noticeably broken.

The attendant viewed media reports the following day about Rosemary Stuart's killing. He reported his suspicions immediately to police and provided them a detailed description of both car and driver.

The Forensics department searched the station's restroom and found samples of Stuart's blood and hair. On midday August 2nd, police tailed a suspicious car matching the description. Once the driver committed a moving violation, he was pulled over.

The paint damage to his vehicle was consistent with their expectations and the driver, Morris Frampton bore an exact likeness to the prime suspect's drawn profile. The Seattle sprinkler system installer was arrested immediately.

The trunk of his vehicle would yield significant evidence including samples of the yellow spongy material and both victims' blood.

Although investigators were certain of his guilt in both

murders, Frampton was exonerated in the death of Peters due to a lack of conclusive evidence. He was found guilty of first-degree murder in Stuart's killing and sentenced to death. The sentence was later modified on appeal to a term of 50 years to life in prison.

Given the violence and savagery accompanying the two murders, it seemed unlikely they were his sole victims.

In 2006, Frampton was charged with the 1976 strangling death of a 48-year-old mother, Agnes Williams, in West Seattle. The arrest was based on DNA matching of the killer found on Williams's body. She had been found beaten and strangled. The slaying had languished unsolved in the cold case files for decades. The reason that brought Williams' and Frampton's life together was never publicly revealed. Detectives were adamant that she was not a prostitute.

Investigators researching the 1976 murder contacted Frampton at the Walla Walla State Penitentiary seeking his cooperation. Five days later, he contacted them and arranged a meeting, accompanied by his attorney. Was he suffering a crisis of conscience after thirty years for his act?

He confessed to a murder, but not Agnes Williams'. He recounted a dreary emotionless recital concerning the killing of Rosemary Stuart, whose name he couldn't remember. He had already been convicted for her murder so the confession was pointless. Frampton was later convicted of second-degree murder for William's death and an additional seventeen years were added to his prison term.

Past 70, Frampton remains interned at the Stafford Creek Corrections Center in Aberdeen. His first eligible parole date will be in 2028; assuming that evidence from additional unsolved killings are not traceable to him.

There would be little surprise if he was not responsible for more victims. The closure for their families and friends would be welcomed. Sadly, most serial killers are incapable of remorse and are typically broken human beings. The probability is high that Frampton will die unrepentant, in prison and carry his depraved secrets with him.

**Morris Frampton Killing Site:
South Park Marina adjacent to Admiral Way Bridge, Seattle**

Robert Lee Yates: Washington's Perpetual *Dead Man Walking* Pleads for Another Unmerited Extension of Life

Robert Lee Yates, Jr. has become the epitome of Washington's *Dead Man Walking*, phraseology used to describe condemned inmates on death row. His life is maze of contradictions, violence and denials. He has exhausted every possible argument and tactic to remain alive. He has succeeded.

Unlike many serial killers originating from abusive homes, Yates grew up in Oak Harbor, a stable middle-class environment. He attended a local Seventh-day Adventist church and exhibited no early signs of emotional imbalance or deviant behavior.

He was hired by the Washington State Department of Corrections in 1975 as a prison guard at the State Penitentiary in Walla Walla. Ironically this location remains his current residence. In 1977, Yates enlisted in the army where he became certified to fly civilian transport airplanes and helicopters. He was stationed at numerous international posts and United National peacekeeping missions in the 1990s. He was commended for his military service with numerous distinctions.

His return to civilian life proved less honorable. He discovered a fresh diversion and obsession. Between 1996 and 1998, Yates was responsible for the documented deaths of at least sixteen prostitutes. His pattern was consistent. He would solicit each one along a notorious stretch of Spokane's *Skid Row* from his 1979 white van. He would usually engage in sex with them inside, sometimes share drugs and then shoot them fatally with a gunshot to the head. The bodies were usually dumped in rural locations with a single exception. One of his victims, Melody Murfin was buried just outside of his residential bedroom window.

His additional victims included Patrick Oliver, Susan Savage, Stacy Hawn, Shannon Zielinski, Patrick Barnes, Heather Hernandez, Jennifer Joseph, Darla Scott, Melinda Mercer, Shawn Johnson, Laurie Wason, Linda Daveys, Michelyn Derning and Connie Ellis.

The life of others had nominal value to Yates, with the exception of his own. He pleaded guilty to thirteen counts of first-degree murder in 2000 to avoid the death penalty. He was sentenced to 408 years in prison.

In 2001, he was charged with two additional murders in Pierce County. He was convicted of first-degree murder for those killings and sentenced to death by lethal injection. He continues to appeal the sentence claiming his earlier plea bargain agreement was *all encompassing*. His arguments were rejected in 2007 and execution date was stayed the following year pending additional appeals.

His defense team filed an innovative claim during 2013 in federal district court. They cited Yates' mental illness and "through no fault of his own…suffered from a severe paraphilic disorder" predisposing him to commit murder. His violent tendencies have not apparently included suicide. During 2015, he once again appealed his conviction. The Washington Supreme Court rejected his claim. And so the circus continues…

Yates' requests for clemency seem as pointless as attempting to make sense of his actions. The continued burden for supporting him becomes one of the strongest arguments to enforce the death penalty. In October 2018, the Washington State Supreme Court abolished the death penalty citing it as unconstitutional.

Robert Lee Yates through his appeals and delays has succeed in extending his own life, but in the end, for what purpose?

**Robert Lee Yates, Jr. Prostitute Pick-up Location:
East Sprague Boulevard, Spokane**

Rodney Alcala: A Beastly Killing Machine Slaying Beauty

The prolific debauchery of serial killer Rodney Alcala has been estimated to have potentially exceeded one hundred female victims spanning a period between 1968 and 1979. He has been convicted for five killings in California, two in New York and is the prime suspect in two Seattle murders.

Unlike serial killer Ted Bundy, who he is often compared with, Alcala has remained mute on identifying his victims or disclosing any potential dumping locations.

Posing under the guise of a fashion photographer, Alcala would lure his victims with promises of intimate photo shoots. Police discovered his personal collection of more than 1,000 sexually explicit photographs leading to the speculation of an expanded victim count. He was reputed to have studied film under director Roman Polanski at New York University.

Initiated with his army enlistment in 1960, he was professionally diagnosed with an antisocial personality disorder and discharged on medical grounds four years later. He would later be appraised as exhibiting a narcissist personality disorder, borderline personality disorder, psychopathic tendencies and sexual sadism.

None of these professional evaluations spared his later victims, which included Cornelia Crilley, Ellen Hover, Jill Barcomb, Georgia Wixted, Charlotte Lamb, Jill Parenteau and Robin Samsoe. He was accused but not tried for the murder of Pamela Lambson and the prime suspect in two Seattle area murders with Antoinette Wittaker and Joyce Gaunt.

On the evening of July 9, 1977, 13-year-old Antoinette Walker, walked out of the front door of the foster home she was living at with an unknown man with long reddish-colored hair. A week later, her body was found fully clothed and propped up on her hands and knees in a corner vacant lot in the Lake City district. Her estimated death was determined to be the week before. She had been stabbed to death. Her mother claimed the death became a low police priority because Walker was African-American.

Joyce Gaunt's body was found at a picnic area at Seward Park. The developmentally disabled teen had been beaten, strangled and sexually assaulted. She was nude and lying on her face with her skull crushed. She'd been living in a group home in the Capitol Hill district and telephoned them around midnight. She abruptly hung up after she was urged to come home.

Alcala could not be directly linked by DNA evidence to either case. There has been speculation he was living in Seattle during the period and the murders and body posings resembled his style. In July 1979, Alcala rented a storage unit in the Shoreline neighborhood. One of his other traced storage lockers in Orange County, California yielded 100s of photo images taken by Alcala. Several of his confirmed murder victims were part of the photo inventory.

The scariest factor about this serial killer is the possibility he may have victims exceeding triple digits.

Alcala possessed the sociopathic capacity to flatter and solicit aided by his handsome appearance. He was cruelly calculated in his manner of executions. He often strangled and then revived his victims from consciousness before ultimately killing them. Many of his victims were stabbed and bludgeoned to death.

He was originally labeled *The Dating Game Killer* because of a 1978 appearance on the identically named television show. He was selected as the winning bachelor contestant but never actually dated his selector due to her aversion towards his erratic behavior.

This behavior became publicly displayed during his third trial when Alcala elected to act as his own attorney. During one memorable five-hour sequence, he made a mockery of the proceedings by assuming the role of interrogator and witness. He asked himself and then answered questions in varying voice tones. He addressed the jury with rambling monotones and introduced unusual evidence that included footage from his *Dating Game* appearance and a segment from Arlo Guthrie's song *Alice's Restaurant*. DNA matching became the primary source of evidence used against him.

The jury convicted him on five-counts of first-degree murder. The proceedings were heightened by the appearance of his first recorded surviving rape and attempted murder victim, Tali Shapiro during the penalty phase. He was sentenced to death and is currently incarcerated at Corcoran State Prison.

Since his conviction, Alcala has periodically resurfaced for public spectacle as subsequent charges have been leveled against him. His once flowing shoulder length hair grayed hideously before being shorn off in prison. Now past seventy, his former alluring appearance has deteriorated into the degeneration matching the horror of his actions.

Antoinette Walker Murder Site: 2024 NE Ninety-Fifth Street, Lake City, Seattle

Joyce Gaunt Body Discovery: Seward Park Picnic Table 5900 Lake Washington Blvd., Seattle

Linda Burfield Hazzard: A Barbaric Medical Practitioner Dispensing Lethal Salt and Water

The American obsession with slimming down was never more abused than by the fasting sanitarium operated by Linda Burfield Hazzard.

Hazzard, who championed a fasting cure, promoted herself as an alternative medical practitioner even though she was merely a licensed osteopathic nurse. She cast herself in the role of innovator, victim and pioneer. She considered herself a champion of women's rights and a direct challenge to the established medical profession. She believed that drugs and surgery were counterproductive to healing.

She was in fact a cruel serial killer and thief masquerading as a medical charlatan, targeting primarily wealthy and gullible patients.

Her operations began with a clinic in Minneapolis. She claimed in a book that she authored that *impure* blood was the cause of all disease. This theory was held commonplace by the medical profession during the Middle Ages and Renaissance. She advocated that eating abstinence would purify and cleanse the body. She alternated excessive water intake with enemas and aggressive massage to rid the body of disease. The result was the body became vacant of nutrients and regressive weight loss developed into anorexia.

Official inquiry and controversy accompanied her methods and prompted her relocation to the Puget Sound region. She and her husband established a clinic inside of a Seattle Capitol Hill office building and purchased forty acres across Puget Sound in Olalla. On that parcel, she established her primary residence and sanitarium there.

In 1911, she admitted two ideal patsy British patients in heiresses Dora and Claire Williamson. Their fates hastened her temporary downfall. Within a month, she had starved both into submission. Each sister was reduced into a painfully emaciated shadow and delirious. Claire died. Hazzard gained control of their considerable fortunes. Dora was rescued but had withered down to sixty pounds.

Hazzard denied that her treatments contributed to Claire's deaths or towards the frightening state of any of the walking skeletons roaming the Olalla grounds. She used her questionable medical credentials to sign Clara's death certificate, citing cirrhosis of the liver as the cause of her death. In most documented cases where other medical professional authenticated her patient's death certificates, starvation was generally the stated cause.

Claire Williamson's death opened her practice to wider public scrutiny and exposure.

The outrage over her extreme abuses reached the British Vice Consul, C. F. Lucien Agassiz based in Tacoma. He was able to compile an extensive list of patients who had died under Hazard's methods. Among the names included Ida Wilcox, Blanche Tindall, Viola Heaton, Mandy Whitney, Eugene Wakelin, Nan Flux, C. A. Harrison, Earl Erdman, Frank Southard and Daisey Hagland, mother of prominent Seattle fish and chips restaurateur Ivar Hagland.

In 1912, she underwent a three-week trial in nearby Port Orchard. Her defense testimony provided her a pulpit for extorting her views on alternative medical practices. Numerous women from the Pacific Northwest flocked to offer their support and admiration, but in vain.

She was found guilty of manslaughter and given a jail sentence of between 2-20 years at the State Penitentiary in Walla Walla. She completed her term and then moved with her husband/partner briefly to New Zealand.

In 1920 she returned to Olalla and resumed her practice despite losing her state medical credentials. Patients and soon-to-be victims continued to check in, but sometimes not out. Despite the adverse publicity and casualties, she was able to construct her dream palatial sanitarium on the site. She named the structure Wilderness Heights. Locals renamed it Starvation Heights and the designation has remained.

The lavish structure included a basement incinerator that served conveniently for disposing of potential autopsy evidence. Her practice gradually waned until the sanitarium burned down in 1935. She died three years later after initiating her own fasting regime for herself.

The irony was as unmistakable as the atrocity of her excruciating murders.

**Starvation Heights Former Location:
12541 Orchard Avenue, Olalla**

**Starvation Heights Seattle Clinic:
1633 Boyston, Seattle**

Warren Forrest: A Heart of Darkness Permanently Confined From Society

Serial killer Warren Forrest began his terror in his early twenties. He was sentenced to life in prison despite an insanity plea for the 1974 death of 20-year-old Krista Blake of Vancouver. He is currently interned at the Washington State Penitentiary in Walla Walla following a stint Monroe Corrections Center.

When he was considered for his first eligible parole date in 2014, the Washington Indeterminate Sentence Review Board denied his request. He remains a prime murder suspect in at least five other missing persons cases. The disappearances occurred between December 1971 and October 1974.

Forrest was an Army veteran and former Clark County parks employee. The graves of multiple victims, all women, have been discovered subsequently in or near Clark County parks.

While in prison, Forrest made statements about being responsible for other victims spread over four states. He confided these disclosures while undergoing mandatory sexual offender treatment. During his treatment periods, he admitted to violent and sadistic behavior that involved rape, stabbing and choking victims to death. As his first parole heating approached, he became unwilling to disclose further pertinent details fearing such candor could sabotage his chances for eventual release. Thankfully the Board had an extended memory.

His first suspected victim was a 16-year old student Jamie Grissim, who disappeared while returning home from Fort Vancouver High School on December 7, 1971.

In August 2017, DNA evidence linked Forrest to two additional murders that had formerly been erroneously attributed to serial killer Ted Bundy. Blood on a weapon used as evidence in a 1974 case against Forrest was matched with an additional victim, 17-year-old Martha Morrison found in a shallow grave in the Dole Valley Area of Clark County. One hundred twenty-feet away the body of 18-year-old Carol Valenzuela was buried in close proximity.

He is also the prime suspect in the abductions and murders of:

Barbara Ann Derry, 18, a Clark College student killed while last seen hitchhiking on Highway 14, east of Vancouver. (February 11, 1972).

A reported kidnap and assault of a 15 year-old hitchhiker living in Ridgefield, who managed to escape after chewing through her bonds. (July 17, 1974).

A 20-year-old university student who was picked up in downtown Portland and transferred to a heavily wooded area. She was sexually assaulted and shot in the chest with hand honed darts from a dart pistol. Miraculously she was able to stagger to a public road where she found assistance. (October 1, 1974).

Gloria Nadine disappeared from downtown Vancouver and her body was recovered near Lacamas Lake (May 31, 1974).

Norma Countryman, 15, barely escaped abduction, beating and her murder in a remote Clark County wooded area. (July 1974)

What lurks in the darkness of Forrest's monstrous soul will never be palatable for public understanding and consumption. Forty years of incarceration may have eliminated his opportunity to commit more terror, but it probably hasn't stilled the beast within. Society has no place for a Warren Forrest. His ability to assimilate back if one day he is released would be inconceivable.

Probable abduction site of Jamie Grissim

Ted Bundy: The Man Who Lived To Kill Women

Theodore Robert Cowell was born at the Elizabeth Lund Home for Unwed Mothers in Burlington, Vermont to Eleanor Louise Cowell. He never knew the identify of his father. He assumed his stepfather Johnny Culpepper Bundy's last name once he was legally adopted.

The Bundy family settled in Tacoma and Eleanor and John had four additional children together. Ted felt remote from his adopted family. He didn't respect his stepfather's intelligence and modest earnings. He would later come to resent his mother's compromise in marrying him and duplicity in lying about his own true heritage.

Numerous biographers have attempted to discern who was the real Ted Bundy. What factors prompted the origins behind his hatred and violence towards women? He assumed the alias of Chris Hagen, Kenneth Misner, Officer Roseland, Richard Burton and Rolf Miller during a homicidal career that was estimated to victimize 30-36 women throughout California, Utah, Florida, Colorado, Oregon, Idaho and Washington between 1974-78. His true victim count may have been substantially higher.

He was never tried, convicted or held accountable for any of his homicides in Washington.

His young female victims perceived Ted Bundy as a disarmingly handsome and charismatic man. He was brazen in approaching many in public places, feigning injury or impersonating an authority figure. Once he had secured their confidence and trust, he overpowered and assaulted them in more secluded locations.

The extent of his debauchery included decapitation and

necrophilia. He evolved within his mind into an efficient killing machine and ultimately considered murder his sole occupation.

Bundy's early Washington formation began with a fascination towards pornography and voyeurism. He felt detached from society and genuine interpersonal relationships.

When he was 14, Tacoma was gripped by the abduction and disappearance of Ann Marie Burr, whose body was never recovered. With his ascending national notoriety, questions arose as to his possible culpability. He denied involvement with her disappearance throughout his life. Nearing his execution, he recited a story about a kidnapping he had committed of a young girl who was buried in an orchard next to her house. The narrative mirrored Ann Burr's disappearance. He would have been intimately familiar with the case due to news reports, but was not necessarily responsible for the act.

On the subject of murder, Ted Bundy spoke habitually in the third person. His words and supposed confessions were never to be fully accepted at face value. His truths were as relative as his views on the value of human life. As a remorseless killer he felt no guilt, shame or responsibility for the reckless damage that he had inflicted.

During high school, he was arrested twice on suspicion of burglary and auto theft. Tacoma was too provincial and small-minded for Bundy's visionary ambitions of himself. He would attend one year at the University of Puget Sound before transferring to the University of Washington (UW) in 1966 to study Chinese.

Bundy nurtured an exalted opinion of his intelligence and

proficiencies, but lacked the initiative and follow-up to achieve his unfocused ambitions. He bounced around for the next three years traveling to Colorado and visiting relatives in Arkansas and Philadelphia. There was speculation that his murderous legacy began during his east coast residence.

In the spring of 1970, he re-enrolled at the UW and earned honors as a psychology major. The following year, he volunteered at the Seattle Suicide Hotline crisis center. There he worked alongside former police officer and aspiring crime writer Ann Rule, who would become his friend and one of his most insightful biographers.

Ann Rule then viewed nothing disturbing about Bundy's personality. She, like many of his future acquaintances described him as *kind*, *solicitous* and *empathetic*. Later she realized that she had been duped by Bundy's appearance and personality. She fittingly titled his biography *The Stranger Beside Me*. In retrospect, she concluded that he was a sadistic sociopath who delighted in other's pain and the control he exerted over his victims.

Despite all of his abominable actions, Bundy always cultivated at least one female advocate. He had the capacity to split his personality and an ability to interpret and manipulate human behavior to his ends.

His appearance of stability solidified in early 1974 when he seemed heading towards an encouraging future in either the legal profession or politics. He then abruptly shifted directions. He broke off serious relationships with two women and began skipping classes. By April, he had dropped out of law school. His focus drifted erratically towards a fresh objective, murder.

There are multiple theories about when and where Bundy first began killing women. His own stories often contradicted themselves. Aside from various suspicions, his earliest documented homicide was committed in 1974 when he was 27-years-old.

On January 4, 1974, he entered the UW campus basement apartment of 18-year-old Karen Sparks (also identified as Joni Lenz or Terri Caldwell). He sexually assaulted and bludgeoned her while she was initially sleeping. She remained in a coma for ten days, but survived with permanent brain damage.

Less than a month later, he broke into another basement bedroom of Lynda Ann Healty, a UW undergraduate. He beat her unconscious and carried her away.

Female college students began disappearing throughout the state and Bundy was the reason. On March 12, Donna Gail Manson (19) disappeared from Evergreen State College in Olympia. On April 17, Susan Elaine Rancourt disappeared while on her way to a movie at Central Washington State College in Ellensburg. Two other students would later come forward to report an encounter with Bundy on the same evening of Rancourt's disappearance.

On May 6, Roberta Kathleen Parks left her dormitory at Oregon State University in Corvallis to have coffee with her friends at the Student Union Building. She never arrived.

The killings continued with a strikingly similar pattern. Bundy would wear a fake arm sling and ask for assistance to carry a load of books to his tan Volkswagen Beetle. When his victim would arrive at the vehicle, he would beat her into unconsciousness and drive her to a remote location.

He was cautious to leave few forensic clues. No one was witness to their final encounter at his vehicle. The bodies were never discovered immediately after the killings. The cases were assigned to missing person status. Bundy had a preferential profile for his victims. They were Caucasian, attractive college students with long hair parted in the middle.

On June 1, Brenda Carol Ball disappeared after leaving the Flame Tavern in Burien. She was last seen talking in the parking lot to a brown-haired man with his arm in a sling. On June 11, UW student Georgann Hawkins vanished walking down a brightly lit block long alley between her boyfriend's dorm room and her sorority house. Afterwards, several witnesses came forward reporting to have seen a man in the alley on crutches with a leg cast, struggling to carry a briefcase.

During this homicidal stretch, he was working at the Washington State Department of Emergency Services in Olympia. Ironically or purposely, the government agency was directly involved in the search for missing women. There he met and dated his future wife, a twice-divorced mother of two. They would marry in 1979 while he was incarcerated in Florida and remained so until 1986.

Reports of the missing women and single confirmed brutal beating paralyzed the Pacific Northwest with fear. Hitchhiking decreased significantly. Bundy's operating tactics were graphically detailed in the media. With no bodies being discovered and minimal crime site evidence, he remained anonymous. He then committed his most audacious public abductions and killings.

During the afternoon of Sunday, July 14, he approached numerous women on the crowded beach at Lake

Sammamish State Park in Issaquah. He was wearing a white tennis outfit with his left arm in a sling and affected a slight British accent. He introduced himself as Ted and asked their assistance in unloading a sailboat from his tan Volkswagen Beetle.

Four women refused and one fled when after accompanying him to his car, saw there was no sailboat. Janice Anne Ott (23) and Denise Naslund (18), four hours later, would follow him to his vehicle and their demise. Both would be murdered that same day. Their skeletal remains would be discovered together on a service road, two miles east of the lake. On that same site, an additional femur and several vertebrae were found and matched to Georgeann Hawkins. Today, a freeway overpass and two steel public artwork sculptures have replaced the former dumping site.

Six months later, forestry students from Green River Community College would discover the skulls and mandibles of Healy, Rancourt, Parks and Ball on an isolated stretch of Taylor Mountain, east of Issaquah. Today, an access road to the site is padlocked and a power station has been constructed nearby. Investigators named the discovery *Bundy's Boneyard*.

In 1974, King County detectives were receiving two hundred tips per day. Several of his acquaintances including Rule reported Bundy as a possible suspect. Detectives dismissed the idea that a clean-cut law student with no criminal record could be responsible.

Before the fall semester of 1974, Bundy was accepted at the University of Utah Law School and moved to Salt Lake City. His Washington trail of horror was complete. He would commit a fresh string of atrocities in Utah, Idaho, Colorado and finally Florida.

Parallel to his move, Washington police were narrowing down their list of potential suspects. This time, Ted Bundy's name surfaced towards the top. Attention towards Bundy's activities accelerated in August 1975 when he failed to pull over for a routine traffic stop in Utah. The officer issuing the citation noted that the Volkswagen front passenger seat was missing and after a search of the vehicle discovered suspicious objects including a ski mask and a second mask fashioned from pantyhose. The policeman also noted a crowbar, handcuffs, trash bags, a coil of rope, an ice pick and other items assumed to be burglary tools. Bundy was released despite the findings.

As Bundy was incapable of holding down steady employment, he frequently resorted to burglary and theft for sustenance.

For the first time, Bundy's name was above the radar and being scrutinized. His apartment was searched, but yielded nothing of substance. Investigators overlooked a collection of Polaroid photographs displaying his victims hidden in a utility room. Shortly afterwards, he sold his Volkswagen to a teenager, thinking he had shed this important piece of potential evidence against him. Utah police impounded the car. In their examination, they began finding evidence traced to multiple murder cases they were currently investigating.

Bundy, however, was not easy prey to confine. Over the next three years, he would be arrested, tried on multiple occasions, serve as his own legal counsel and escape twice in Colorado while in confinement. Wanted and desperate, Bundy followed a circuitous route to Chicago, Michigan, Atlanta and finally Florida.

In Florida, he might have remained incognito had he avoided his criminal past. He confided in prison that his intention was to revert to a life of legitimate employment and abstinence from additional criminal activities. He abandoned his intentions within a week after his arrival.

On January 14, 1978, he attacked four women, killing two at a Florida State University Sorority House. Over the next month, broke, paranoid of discovery and driving a stolen car, Bundy continued his mayhem throughout the state including the killing of a 12-year-old Lake City student. He was finally arrested in Pensacola after being pulled over and attempting to resist arrest.

His trial for the Sorority House murders proved a personal debacle as he attempted to handle his own defense, despite the presence of five court-appointed attorneys. His reputation now had become international news. Over 250 reporters from five continents covered the trial. His trial was the first to be televised nationally. He refused a 75-year prison term plea bargain assuming that he was clever enough to fool a jury. He miscalculated his legal abilities and in July 1979 was convicted of two murders, three attempted murders and two burglary counts. The trial judge sentenced him to death.

Six months later, he was tried for the Lake City murder. In February 1980, Bundy was sentenced to death by electrocution.

Following his murder trials, Bundy became a popular interview. He was vaulted into the spotlight as the world's most articulate and recognized serial killer. He relished the attention, but confessed to nothing. He remained confident that the appeal process would secure his release.

Bundy took great satisfaction in elevating his ego to elite expertise on the subject of serial killing. He offered to share his opinions with Washington investigators during their hunt for the Green River killer. He was interviewed and offered some insight into Gary Ridgway's necrophilia. Ridgway would not be arrested until seventeen years later due to forensic DNA matching.

While on death row, he was attacked and reportedly raped by a gang of fellow inmates. He incurred a disciplinary infraction by contacting another high-profile criminal, John Hinckley, Jr. who had wounded President Ronald Reagan in 1981.

Bundy's supporters and legal team exhausted every possible appeal and stay of executive before a fixed execution date was set for January 24, 1989. With no further incentive to deny his crimes and a strategy to potentially delay his execution, he began to speak candidly to investigators. He confessed in the third person to many of the murders where he was the prime suspect.

He elaborated details right up to the end of his life, confident that his continued exposures would buy him additional time. Once again, his supposition was incorrect. He was executed as scheduled at 7:16 a.m. and cremated in Gainesville. His ashes were scattered over an undisclosed location in the Washington Cascade Range, a terrain he revered and hiked often.

During his incarcerations, Ted Bundy underwent multiple psychiatric examinations. No one could conclusively pinpoint the reasons behind his obsession towards killing young women. His diagnosis included bipolar disorder, multiple personality disorder, narcissistic personality disorder, antisocial personality disorder, sociopath and psychopath. All may have may have been partially or entirely correct. Bundy delighted in toying with individuals attempting to make sense of his life.

At best, he may have shed a glimpse into a soul of complete darkness. His insight into the thinking process of a serial killer has doubtlessly been employed into the profiling efforts of law enforcement agencies.

If ever a man lived to make murder his primary occupation and life obsession, it was unquestionably Ted Bundy.

**Hometown Residence:
658 Skyline, Tacoma**

University of Washington Residence: 4143 12th Avenue NE, Seattle

**Jodi Lenz Assault:
4325 8th Street NE, Seattle**

**Lynda Ann Healy's Murder Site:
5517 NE 12th Street, Seattle**

**Georgann Hawkin's Abduction Site:
Alleyway Behind 1617 47th Avenue NE, Seattle**

Brenda Ball's Last Sighted Location: Former Flame Tavern, 12803 South Ambaum Blvd, Burien

Issaquah Service Road Dumping Ground: Two Steel Flower Sculptures at the intersection of Highlands Drive NE and Interstate 90

Boneyard: Taylor Mountain, Rattlesnake Road SE, Issaquah (East of Highway 18)

Kenneth Bianchi: Over Forty Years of Time Remaining Stationary For An Unrepentant Killer

Kenneth Bianchi began life troubled and has subsequently spent the majority of his life incarcerated. He was born in 1951 to an alcoholic prostitute in Rochester, New York who gave him up for adoption two weeks after he was born.

From an early age, Bianchi exhibited troubling personality defects including compulsive lying, inattentiveness, involuntary urination problems, seizures, outbreaks of sudden anger and trance-like daydreams where his eyes would roll back into his head. His IQ was rated above average, but he did poorly in school and clashed with his teachers primarily due to his inactivity.

The instability behind being adopted deepened when his father died suddenly from pneumonia when he was thirteen. He barely graduated from high school and married his girlfriend shortly afterwards. The marriage ended after eight months when she left him without explanation.

He remained in Rochester until 1977 working at menial jobs and finally as a jewelry store security guard. His theft of jewelry and valuables was often transferred to girlfriends and prostitutes as gifts. Between 1971 and 1973, a series of unsolved *Alphabet* murders plagued Rochester resulting in three young girls being kidnapped, raped and murdered. Bianchi denied involvement, but was considered a prime suspect.

He relocated to Los Angeles in 1977 and began spending time with his older cousin Angelo Buono where they masqueraded as undercover police officers. They reportedly operated as pimps, but soon were trawling the streets at night with fake law enforcement badges. They would order girls and women between the ages of 12 to 28 into their car and take them to Buomo's home before torturing and murdering them. For two years they terrorized Los Angeles and became known as the *Hillside Strangler*.

During their span of terror, Bianchi and Buono experimented with various macabre means of killing including lethal injection, electric shock and carbon monoxide poisoning. Bianchi was by far the least discreet of the pair. He applied for a position with the Los Angeles Police Department and accompanied officers on ride-alongs while they were searching for the *Hillside Strangler*. He eventually attracted attention from police investigators and they began questioning him regarding the killings.

When Buono learned of these events, he became infuriated with Bianchi and threatened to kill him if he did not relocate to distant Bellingham. Bianchi did in May 1978. He found employment as a security guard, but his mania for killing returned on January 11, 1979. He lured a co-worker, Karen Mandic and her roommate Karen Wilder, both college students, into a ranch-style house overlooking Chuckanut Bay in Fairhaven. He had promised each $100 if they would occupy the residence for two hours while the security-alarm system was being repaired. His company had been hired to monitor the property while the owner was vacationing with his wife in Europe.

During the evening at approximately 7:00 p.m. the two women drove over together to the property to meet with Bianchi. Upon arrival, he forced his co-worker down the stairs in front of him and then strangled her. He followed the same routine with Wilder. Without Buono's assistance, he left scattered clues at the murder site.

Mandic had left her job for a two-hour dinner break to meet Bianchi. When she didn't return, her boss telephoned a friend who worked at the Western Washington University Security department regarding her strange disappearance. Mandic had confided with another friend who worked in the same office regarding her offer and intended rendezvous.

The Bellingham police were immediately notified and the search for the two women and Mandic's green 1998 Mercury Bobcat hatchback began. The police contacted Bianchi's security firm due to their contracted arrangement with the homeowners. They spoke with Bianchi at 2:30 a.m. to question his whereabouts. He lied and indicated that he'd attended a sheriff's office reserve class earlier. The alibi fell apart when his commander confirmed that he hadn't attended the class. The ever-deceitful Bianchi modified his story to indicate that he had gone driving alone in the countryside.

The next morning when the women did not attend classes, a full-scale search was conducted resulting in the late afternoon discovery of the Mercury Bobcat at the end of an undeveloped cul-de-sac. The bodies had been hurriedly stuffed into the car's back seat. The medical examiner confirmed the deaths by strangulation after conducting the autopsies.

Bianchi's security company dispatcher contacted him and ordered him to report to the security guard's shack at the Port of Bellingham's South Terminal. Upon arrival, he was taken into custody for questioning. It was the final taste of freedom he would ever experience. Karen Wilder's coat was discovered twenty feet away from the guard shack behind some pipes.

As the investigation of Kenneth Bianchi intensified, incriminating pieces began to assemble into place. Evidence and eyewitnesses placed the security company truck and perpetrator at the crime site. In the process of doing a background check on Bianchi and his Los Angeles years, detectives were directed to the head of the Hillside Strangler Task Force that was in the process of investigating 13 female murders since October 1977. Within two days of the lead detective's arrival to Bellingham, evidence found on Bianchi linked him to the Hillside Strangler case and the direct association with his cousin Angelo Buono.

The judge refused to release Bianchi from custody and established a bail of $150,000 considering him a flight risk.

On Friday, January 26, 1979 Bianchi was formally charged with two counts of first-degree murder in the deaths of Mandic and Wilder. He initially pled *not guilty* and by the end of March modified it to *not guilty by reason of insanity*. Meanwhile the evidence was mounting against the two cousins in Los Angeles. On May 9th, the Los Angeles District Attorney charged Bianchi with his direct involvement in five of ten confirmed murders. Conviction would qualify Bianchi for the gas chamber.

Over the next months, Bianchi underwent a competency hearing in Washington that involved hypnosis. Play acting through multiple personalities, the charade became irrelevant when he abandoned his insanity defense and pled guilty to two life terms without the possibility of parole. One of the conditions for removing the death penalty option involved his testifying against his cousin at Buono's upcoming trial.

Bianchi with his characteristic incompetence attempted to discredit himself and confuse the jury as a witness. The evidence was insurmountable and both were found guilty. Buono was sentenced to ten consecutive life sentences and Bianchi five on top of his preexisting Washington convictions.

Since his internment, Kenneth Bianchi has been neither a model prisoner nor passive spectator to his determined fate. He attempted to recruit a jail admirer to simulate similar strangulations even to the point of passing on to her a semen specimen in the fingertip of a latex glove. The plan was idiotically hatched to demonstrate that the true killer was still at large. In September 1980, she attempted to strangle a woman in a motel room after an evening of drinking, luring her inside with the promise of cocaine. She nearly succeeded, but was physically overpowered by her potential victim. She was labeled by the press as the *Copycat Strangler*.

He has filed nearly twenty legal petitions regarding his case in the futile glimmer that one day he may be released. All have been denied. He has sued various individuals based on a perception of being unfairly maligned or taken advantage of financially by the use of his image. He remains imprisoned at the Washington State Penitentiary, which has been his home for over four decades. Should he miraculously complete his Washington terms, he will be transferred to California to serve those.

Buono died of a heart attack while incarcerated. Bianchi has become the perfect embodiment of why society needs a death penalty. He could conceivably live another two to three decades, self-absorbed and unrepentant for crimes that he still denies involvement with.

**Karen Mandic and Karen Wilder Murder Site:
334 Bayside Road, Bellingham**

Author, photographer and visual artist Marques Vickers was born in 1957 in Vallejo, California. He graduated from Azusa Pacific University in Los Angeles and became the Public Relations and Executive Director for the Burbank, California Chamber of Commerce between 1979-84.

Professionally, he has operated travel, apparel, wine, rare book and publishing businesses. His paintings and sculptures have been exhibited in art galleries, private collections and museums in the United States and Europe. He has previously lived in the Burgundy and Languedoc regions of France and currently lives in the South Puget Sound region of Western Washington.

He has written and published over one hundred books spanning a diverse variety of subjects including true crime, international travel, social satire, wine production, architecture, history, fiction, auctions, fine art, poetry and photojournalism.

He has two daughters, Charline and Caroline who reside in Europe.

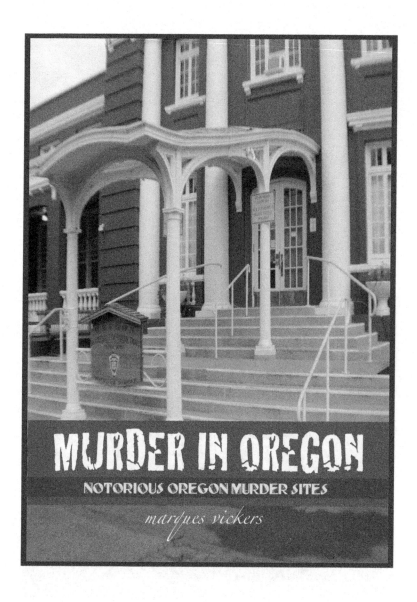

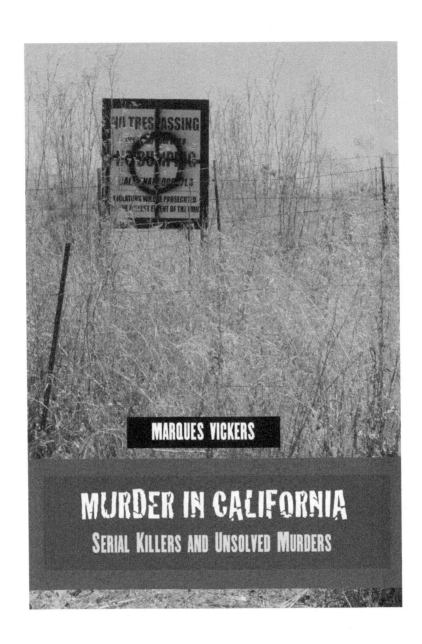

Made in United States
Orlando, FL
15 May 2023